Spain and the Plains

Spain and the Plains

Myths and Realities of Spanish Exploration and Settlement on the Great Plains

Edited by Ralph H. Vigil, Frances W. Kaye,
and John R. Wunder

University Press of Colorado

The University Press of Colorado is a cooperative publishing enterprise
supported, in part, by Adams State College, Colorado State University,
Fort Lewis College, Mesa State College, Metropolitan State College of Denver,
University of Colorado, University of Northern Colorado, University of Southern
Colorado, and Western State College of Colorado.

The paper used in this publication meets the minimum requirements
of the American National Standard for Information Sciences—Permanence
of Paper for Printed Library Materials. ANSI Z39.48—1984.

∞

Library of Congress Cataloging-in-Publication Data

Spain and the Plains: Myths and realities of Spanish exploration
    and settlement on the Great Plains / edited by Ralph H. Vigil,
    Frances W. Kaye, John R. Wunder
        p.   cm.
    Includes bibliographical references and index.
    ISBN 0-87081-352-8 (cloth)
    1. Great Plains—Discovery and exploration—Spanish.
    2. Southwest, New—History—To 1848.
    3. Spaniards—Great Plains—History.
    I. Vigil, Ralph H. (Ralph Harold), 1932-   .
    II. Kaye, Frances W.   III. Wunder, John R.
    F799.S69   1994
    978' .01—dc20
                                                        94-27335
                                                        CIP

10   9   8   7   6   5   4   3   2   1

For Frank and Rafael
Joel
Amanda and Nell

Contents

Maps

Maps for *Spain and the Plains* were prepared and produced by Brad Bays, Department of Geography, Northwestern State University (Louisiana), and are used by permission.

Preface

In April 1989 the Center for Great Plains Studies hosted the first-ever conference devoted to the Latino experience on the Great Plains. The symposium was part of the center's continuing commitment to encourage scholarship in areas previously ignored or untouched and to document the complex ethnic diversity of the Great Plains.

Essays presented at the symposium, including four found in this volume, were published in the *Great Plains Quarterly*. A special issue of the *Quarterly*, Number 10 (Spring 1990), was devoted to the Hispanic presence on the Great Plains, and it included an introduction by Miguel A. Carranza, associate professor of sociology and ethnic studies at the University of Nebraska–Lincoln, who also chaired the program committee for the symposium.

The editors of this volume wish to express their thanks to Dr. Carranza and members of the program committee of the University of Nebraska–Lincoln. The editors are also extremely appreciative of those who made conference presentations, including Jorge Bustamante (El Colegio de la Frontera Norte, Tijuana, Mexico), Juan Garcia (University of Arizona), Estevan T. Flores (University of Colorado–Boulder), James Gunnerson (University of Nebraska–Lincoln), Louise Año Nuevo Kerr (University of Illinois–Chicago), Richard Santillan (California State Polytechnic University–Pomona), Dennis Nodín Valdés (University of Wisconsin–Madison), Philip Baker (South Dakota State University), Reed Anderson (Miami University), Jan Wahl (Nebraska Wesleyan University), Neil F. Foley (University of Michigan), Mario C. Compean (University of Wisconsin–Madison), Benjamin Ávila (University of Nebraska–Kearney), Ella Ochoa (Nebraska Association of Farmworkers), Laura Garza Kerzee (Nebraska State Mexican–American Commission), Richard W. Griffin (Pan American University), Anne B.W. Effland (Iowa State University), Robert Mossman (St. Gregory High School, Tucson, Arizona), Evelyn Haller (Doane College), Fred Pinnegar (University of Arizona), Michael W. Smith (Oklahoma State University), and Douglas Heffington (University of Oklahoma).

This volume is truly the product of three editors. We are extremely grateful to the Center for Great Plains Studies staff members who assisted in the preparation of this book, particularly Lori Gourama, Sharon Bays, Linda J. Ratcliffe, Karen Morin, and Lynn M. Cawthra. In addition, we express our gratitude to Paul Kelly, history Ph.D student, University of Nebraska–Lincoln, for his research on the timeline; Brad Bays, Instructor in Geography, Northwestern State University (Louisiana), for his maps; and Amanda Jaye Wunder, recent history graduate, Wesleyan University, for her index.

Ralph H. Vigil, Frances W. Kaye, and *John R. Wunder*
Lincoln, NE

Acknowledgments

The following chapters have been printed in similar form in the *Great Plains Quarterly*, edited by Frances W. Kaye and published by the Center for Great Plains Studies, University of Nebraska–Lincoln:

Chapter 3: "Spanish Exploration and the Great Plains in the Age of Discovery" by Ralph H. Vigil was published as "Spanish Exploration and the Great Plains in the Age of Discovery: Myth and Reality," *Great Plains Quarterly* 10 (Winter 1990): 3–17.

Chapter 4: "Coronado and Quivira" by Waldo R. Wedel was published as "Coronado, Quivira, and Kansas: An Archeologist's View," *Great Plains Quarterly* 10 (Summer 1990): 139–51.

Chapter 5: "An Uninviting Land: El Llano Estacado, 1534–1821" by Félix D. Almaráz, Jr., was published as "An Uninviting Wilderness: The Plains of West Texas, 1534–1821," *Great Plains Quarterly* 12 (Summer 1992): 169–80.

Chapter 6: "The Villasur Expedition and the Segesser Hide Paintings" by Thomas E. Chávez was published as "The Segesser Hide Paintings: History, Discovery, Art," *Great Plains Quarterly* 10 (Spring 1990): 96–109.

Chapter 7: "The Genízaro Experience in Spanish New Mexico" by Russell M. Magnaghi was published as "Plains Indians in New Mexico: The Genízaro Experience," *Great Plains Quarterly* 10 (Spring 1990): 86–95.

Spain and the Plains

1
An Introduction to Spain and the Great Plains

Ralph H. Vigil and John R. Wunder

As subjects of literature and history, the Hispanics who explored the Great Plains are less well known than the Europeans who immigrated there in the nineteenth century. The major explanation for their invisibility in historical studies of the Great Plains (also known as the Central Plains or the Midwest) is that Mexican Americans and other Hispanics are one of the region's newest immigrant groups. Another reason for the neglect of Hispanics in histories of the Plains has to do with the polarization of the Hispanic heritage, or what may be called the artificial racial dualism between Spaniards of an earlier period and Mexican Americans of today.[1]

Originally one heritage unified in time, Hispanic cultural and racial traditions have since been alternately enshrined and denigrated. The counterpoint of the White Legend, which emphasizes Spain's civilizing mission and the humanitarian aspects of its colonial policy, is the Black Legend of Spanish cruelty, injustice, and despoilment. But whether emphasizing the romantic, heroic, and civilizing side of Spanish settlement or the materialistic and brutal aspects of conquest, historians have usually considered Spaniards to be Europeans — in other words, white and Christian.

In contrast, both friends and foes of recent Mexican and Latin American immigrants and the Hispanos indigenous to the Southwest have viewed them as "Indian in physique, temperament, character, and mentality."[2] Advocates such as Carey McWilliams simply stated that they were "more Indian in racial origin, and perhaps in culture, than they are Spanish." However, a more developed image that appears in some novels and in testimony by farmers who wished to exploit them portrays Mexicans as docile children of the earth, "quite content with their status."[3] As Joan W. Moore observes, this image follows "a theme still strong in American literature about the American Indian," that of the noble savage "who follows the simple life without neurotic complications."[4]

Other self-serving stereotypes may be found. Nativists in the 1920s generally considered Mexicans to be a "degenerate and inferior people, incapable of assimilation or good citizenship."[5] In his landmark history *The Great Plains,* published in 1931, Walter Prescott Webb contrasted Coronado's three hundred "gentlemen on horseback," who "had at their heels the daring and courageous sons of Spain, pure Spaniards brought up in the school of chivalry," with the eighteenth-century soldier on the northern frontier of New Spain, "unfit for the task he had in hand."[6] Webb claimed that the Spanish northern frontier came to depend "more and more on an Indian population and on the mixture that resulted from the mingling of the blood of Spaniards, Negroes, and Indians with the Indians predominating." He concluded that this "mixture of races meant in time that the common soldier in the Spanish service came largely from [P]ueblo or sedentary Indian stock, whose blood, when compared with that of the Plains Indians, was as ditch water. It took more than a little mixture of Spanish blood and the mantle of Spanish service to make valiant soldiers of the timid [P]ueblo Indians who were born in fear of the raiders from the Plains."[7]

Webb, a native Texan and an admirer of "the pure American stock," went on to claim that the "West, or the Great Plains," was a region inhabited by "the so-called typical American of English or Scotch or Scotch-Irish descent." According to Webb, the "foreign element" was represented by Germans in Illinois and Iowa and by Scandinavians in Montana, but other Europeans and Africans were not attracted to the arid Plains, whereas "the Chinese remained on the Pacific coast and the Mexican element stayed close to the southern border."[8] In addition to differentiating between "pure" (and therefore "superior") Spaniards and "racially mixed" (and therefore inferior) "so-called Spaniards," Webb in *The Texas Rangers* (1935) stated that Mexicans were volatile in temperament, cruel in nature, no keepers of promises, inferior to the Comanches, and wholly unequal to Texans as warriors.[9]

Webb's views concerning the abilities of the soldiers charged with protecting the "defensive salients" extending to the frontier of New Spain's viceroyalty, the people in the Spanish expeditions on the Plains, and the early settlers are challenged by other scholars' studies,[10] both in this volume and elsewhere. The myths set forth in Webb's scholarship and the stereotypes found in today's world are the subject of considerable comment in these studies.

The topic of this volume, Spain and the Plains, has been ignored in the histories. Occasionally a section of a volume is devoted to the topic, but that is the exception rather than the rule. In April 1989, the Center for Great Plains Studies hosted the first conference ever devoted to the Hispanic presence on the Great Plains, and most of the essays that follow were presented at that time. Similarly, the first issue of a scholarly journal ever devoted to this topic was published by the Center in its Spring 1990 *Great Plains Quarterly* issue.

The timeline and essays that follow consider the myth and reality of the Spanish presence on the Great Plains. Exploration, diplomacy, military conflict, relationships with Native Americans, searches for gold, missionary zeal, adjustments to environment, and early settlement are the topics presented. A concluding epilogue places Spain and the Plains within a comprehensive four-hundred-year perspective.

Notes

1. Carey McWilliams, *North from Mexico: The Spanish-Speaking People of the United States,* revised edition, updated by Matt S. Meier (New York: Praeger, 1990), p. 29.

2. Ibid., p. 7. McWilliams is mistaken in his idea that the Spanish-speaking people are perhaps more culturally Indian than Spanish. Indeed, if we consider language, which is intimately related to culture, we can only conclude that traces of Indian culture are slim. In the early part of the century, the Spanish-speaking people of New Mexico and southern Colorado used fewer than one hundred Nahuatl words and not more than a score of words from the languages of the Pueblo Indians and surrounding Indian nations. See Aurelio M. Espinosa, "The Spanish Language in New Mexico and Southern Colorado," *Publication No. 16 of the Historical Society of New Mexico* (Santa Fe: New Mexico Printing Co., 1911), pp. 1–37. For the difference between Hispanos (New Mexicans) and Hispanics, see Nancie

L. González, *The Spanish-American of New Mexico* (Albuquerque: University of New Mexico Press, 1969), p. 187. Although "Hispano" usually refers to native New Mexicans, it also means "a person of Spanish or Indo-Hispanic descent native to the American Southwest (Rubén Cobos, *A Dictionary of New Mexico and Southern Colorado Spanish* (Santa Fe: Museum of New Mexico Press, 1983), p. 83; Richard L. Nostrand, *The Hispano Homeland* (Norman: University of Oklahoma Press, 1992); and Alfredo Jiménez Núñez, *Los hispanos de Nuevo Mexico: Contribución a una antropología de la cultura Hispana en USA* (Seville: Publicaciones de la Universidad de Seville, 1974). "Hispanic" is a newly coined federal term including all Spanish-surnamed people and is synonymous with "Latino."

3.   Joan W. Moore with Harry Pachon, *Mexican Americans* (Englewood Cliffs, NJ: Prentice-Hall, 1976), p. 5.

4.   Ibid., p. 4.

5.   Rodolfo Acuña, *Occupied America: The Chicano's Struggle Toward Liberation* (San Francisco: Canfield Press, 1972), p. 140.

6.   Walter Prescott Webb, *The Great Plains* (New York: Grosset & Dunlap, 1931), pp. 125–26.

7.   Ibid., p. 126.

8.   Ibid., p. 509.

9.   Walter Prescott Webb, *The Texas Rangers* (Cambridge, MA: Houghton Mifflin, 1935), p. 14.

10.   Webb's ideas concerning the Texas Rangers and Mexican character have been corrected by Americo Paredes, who notes that "not all Rangers lived up to their reputation as a fearless breed of men" and that attitudes and beliefs about Mexicans based upon their actions at the Alamo, Mier, and Goliad later served as a convenient excuse to rationalize the taking of Mexicans' lives and property. See Americo Paredes, *"With a Pistol in His Hand," A Border Ballad and Its Hero* (Austin: University of Texas Press, 1958), p. 19. See also Ralph H. Vigil, "The New Borderlands History: A Critique," *New Mexico Historical Review* 48 (Number 3, 1973): 189–208.

✝

2

Spanish Exploration in the Great Plains: A Timeline

Ralph H. Vigil and John R. Wunder

Spanish exploration and subsequent settlement in the center of North America was extensive. Few historians recognize the complexity and breadth of coverage of this Spanish presence. Beginning in the 1530s with Alvar Núñez Cabeza de Vaca's travels, which touched the southern Plains, Spain continued to penetrate the heartland, reaching as far north as present-day Nebraska in 1720, when a military expedition led by Don Pedro de Villasur was defeated by Otos and Pawnees. Thereafter, Spain concentrated its settlement and exploration efforts in the southern Plains of Texas, Colorado, Oklahoma, and New Mexico. Through nearly four centuries of continuous activity, Spaniards joined the dynamic history of the peoples of the Great Plains.

1494

Following a contract between Spain's Catholic monarchs and Christopher Columbus for the "Enterprise of the Indies" and the discovery of islands "and even mainlands" where no one had previously sailed, the papacy responded to the Portuguese Crown's charges of Spanish encroachment in the Atlantic region. Pope Alexander VI issued a series of bulls that finally established a boundary 370 leagues west of the Azores and Cape Verde Islands, giving Castile exclusive rights of discovery and possession west of this line.

1519

Following the settlement of Hispaniola and the conquest of the Greater Antilles and Florida, other explorers made known that vast extent of the lands to the west. One explorer, Alonso Álvarez de Pineda, coasted the shores of Florida and the Gulf of Mexico as far west as Texas in search of a strait leading to Cathay. At Veracruz Pineda's fleet learned that Hernán Cortés had already taken possession of what would become New Spain.

1528–36

Following the ill-fated expedition of Pánfilo de Narváez to Florida, Alvar Núñez Cabeza de Vaca (the expedition's treasurer) and various survivors constructed makeshift boats and were cast ashore on an island off the Texas coast near present-day Galveston. The Spaniards were quickly reduced from eighty to fifteen. After more than a year of harsh treatment and constant hunger on the Island of Ill Fate and the mainland, Cabeza de Vaca escaped from his Indian captors, possibly Karankawas, and traveled west with three other survivors among Coahuiltecan-speaking Indians in search of Pánuco, Mexico, founded by Hernán Cortés. They took a long and circuitous journey over the southern Texas plains and across the Río Grande. At Nuevo León, the party went inland and met Indians at La Junta de los Ríos in the vicinity of present-day Presidio, Texas. They then ascended the Río Grande on the Texas side, recrossed the river, and turned westward toward the Pacific. Cabeza de Vaca's party met twenty-three Indian groups between Galveston Island and the Río Grande. His account also states that he saw buffalo three times and that the survivors were given buffalo and cotton robes on their journey. This information, found in the 1555 edition of the narrative, is confirmed by the royal chronicler Gonzalo Fernández de Oviedo, who states that in 1547 Cabeza de Vaca told him of the "cattle" who came from the direction of the north as far as the coast of Florida, a distance of more than four hundred leagues.

Cabeza de Vaca's tale of adventure and his sighting of traces of gold, "precious stones" (malachite?), lead, and other metals impressed Viceroy Antonio de Mendoza and the Franciscan friars and led to the idea that Seven Cities of Gold in the north were ready for the taking.

The Franciscan friar Marcos de Niza was sent north to investigate the mystery.

1539

Fray Marcos was accompanied by a lay brother of the Franciscan order and Estevan (Estevanico), the blackamoor survivor of the Narváez expedition. Acting as Niza's guide and bedecked with quantities of turquoise and feathers, Estevan, followed by Indian women given him by the Pima and Opata Indians, reached the Zuñi settlement of Hawikuh before Fray Marcos. The Zuñis killed him because they thought him to be a spy and because they resented his asking them for turquoise and women.

After Estevan's death, Fray Marcos fled south and reported that he had seen Cíbola (Zuñi), a pueblo of fine appearance larger than the city of Mexico. His tale of "another Mexico" and sermons by the Franciscan friars of populous cities rich in gold and precious stones allowed Viceroy Mendoza to rid his region of some unruly elements hungry for wealth and glory.

1540–42

An expedition commissioned by Viceroy Mendoza and commanded by Francisco Vázquez de Coronado consisted of 230 mounted men, an infantry detachment of 62 men, perhaps 1,300 Indian allies, 1,000 horses, and about 500 pack animals. Fray Marcos served as chief guide but returned to Mexico after the army's capture of Cíbola on 7 July 1540. Coronado's quest for golden cities and the land of Quivira was a failure, but this expedition and that of Hernando de Soto (1539–43) gave the European world a treasure trove of geographical information about what would become the southwestern and southeastern parts of the United States. Coronado traveled through the present states of Arizona and New Mexico, the Texas Panhandle, and the Great Plains of Oklahoma and Kansas. News of native societies of the lower Colorado River, the Sonora desert, New Mexico and Arizona, and the Great Plains raised religious leaders' hopes for future conversions, although no golden cities were found. Soto's expedition wandered for three years through the future states of Florida, Georgia, North and South Carolina, Tennessee, Alabama, Mississippi, Arkan-

1590–93

The 1582–83 Espejo-Beltrán expedition rekindled the dream of great wealth in the north and was joined to the continuing desire of the friars to convert Pueblo Indians. Another incentive for the Crown's wish to settle New Mexico was the rumor that Sir Francis Drake, in the first English circumnavigation of the world (1577–80), had discovered the long-sought transcontinental strait north of Mexico. Espejo and various other applicants were considered before Don Juan de Oñate, a Zacatecas silver king, was awarded a contract for the settlement of New Mexico in 1595.

Before royal confirmation of Oñate's request was given, two unauthorized expeditions into New Mexico were made. The first, in 1590, was led by Gaspar Castaño de Sosa, the lieutenant governor of Nuevo León. This expedition of 170 settlers was forced to return to Coahuila and Nuevo León after Capt. Juan Morlete, the viceroy's agent, arrested its leader. Castaño de Sosa, sentenced to exile in Asia for six years, was killed by galley slaves on the trip.

The second illegal expedition was led by Capt. Francisco Leyva de Bonilla and may have gone as far north as the Purgatory River in present-day southeastern Colorado before it turned eastward into Kansas. The expedition may have continued on to the Platte River in Nebraska. Somewhere on the Plains, Antonio Gutiérrez de Humaña killed Leyva. According to an Indian survivor of the expedition who later returned to New Mexico, the rest of the party was killed by Indians. A reminder of this expedition is found in the name of the Purgatory River, *el río de las ánimas perdidas en purgatorio* ("River of souls lost in Purgatory"); the river was later rechristened by latecomers and is also known as the Picket Wire.

1598–1610

Don Juan de Oñate expended more than 600,000 pesos in the settlement of New Mexico. He arrived with 129 soldier-settlers and their families, 7,000 head of stock, and 83 wagons loaded with goods. Instead of continuing down the Conchos River, Oñate opened a new trail direct to the Río Grande, reaching today's El Paso del Norte in April 1598. In July, at present Santo Domingo, he received the submission of the chiefs of seven provinces and then continued north and established his headquarters at the village of Okhe (San Juan Pueblo).

In 1599 he moved the Spaniards to San Gabriel Pueblo and built a new church and irrigation ditches. On August 18 Oñate welcomed the colonists, who had followed behind in a wagon train.

After putting down a mutiny of some of the settlers, who cursed the poverty of the land and planned to desert the settlement, Oñate prepared for the winter by sending his nephew Vicente de Zaldívar east with sixty men to procure meat. In September, Zaldívar and his party set out for the Plains and met the Apache Vaqueros. On the present western boundary of Texas, Zaldívar obtained a great amount of meat and tallow and attempted but failed to bring back several buffalo calves he captured. Meanwhile, Franciscan friars began the work of conversion, and Oñate prepared to explore westward as far as the Gulf of California and eastward in search of Quivira.

In October Oñate left another nephew, Juan de Zaldívar, in charge at San Juan and set out in search of the sea to the west of his kingdom. On this expedition he visited Ácoma — where, he later learned, the local residents had planned to kill him — and then went on to Zuñi. Part of his party also met a group of Cruzado Indians, perhaps today's Yavapai, in the vicinity of the San Francisco Peaks.

By now Vicente de Zaldívar had returned to San Juan, leaving Juan de Zaldívar free to join Oñate. On the way to join his uncle with thirty men, Juan stopped at Ácoma and attempted to trade Spanish goods for corn flour, and he and ten of his companions were killed. In response, Oñate commissioned Vincente to attack Ácoma before the revolt spread to other pueblos. In early 1599 hundreds of Ácoma Indians were killed; those who were captured were sentenced to servitude. Captured males over the age of twenty-five were mutilated before being sentenced.

In June 1601, after the colony received reinforcements, Oñate led an expedition of more than seventy men in search of Quivira. Beyond the Pecos River the Spaniards crossed the Plains to the Canadian River, followed its course across the level land, turned northeast to the Cimarron River, and found buffalo thirty-six days' distance from Galisteo Pueblo. When the expedition came to the vicinity of the Arkansas River, it encountered a tipi village of some five thousand Indians. These Indians, called Escanjaques, were enemies of the Wichitas (the "Quivirans" Coronado had encountered sixty years earlier). They told Oñate of the massacre of Jumanos, Indians located further south, allegedly carried out by the people of Quivira. Some of the Escanjaque warriors traveled with Oñate to the Arkansas River, where the party met the Quivirans, a painted-cheeked and tattooed people living in huge grass houses in the vicinity of present-day Wichita, Kansas. On the return trip from these settlements, Escanjaque warriors attacked the Spaniards and wounded many.

On his return to San Gabriel on November 24, Oñate found that many of the colonists, fed up with the scarcity of food and the failure to find rich mines after four years of exploration, had left for Santa Bárbara. Oñate's failure to find another Zacatecas in New Mexico and the disgruntlement of colonists who resented his rule eventually brought about his recall. In 1610 the first royal governor of New Mexico, Don Pedro de Peralta, moved the capital to Santa Fe.

1629

Fray Juan de Salas departed Santa Fe with a few soldiers and visited the Jumanos in the vicinity of the Concho and Colorado rivers. Trade relations between New Mexico and these Indians continued for the rest of the seventeenth century. Meanwhile, rumors of Quivira, Gran Teguayo, and a rich kingdom of the Tejas Indians gave Spanish officials hope that more than buffalo hides and freshwater pearls would be found east of El Paso and north of Santiago de Monclova, founded in Coahuila in 1687.

1655–75

In these years Spanish soldiers crossed the Río Grande, and Fray Juan Larios and Fray Manuel de la Cruz of the Franciscan order began work in a new missionary field on the Coahuila frontier. In 1675 a small party of Spaniards led by Fernando del Bosque, lieutenant governor of Coahuila province, and Father Larios crossed the Río Grande. The expedition found wide plains and plentiful water and visited tribes who hunted the buffalo. Many Indian nations asked for instruction in Christian doctrine. In 1676 the bishop of Guadalajara expressed as a goal the establishment of missions north of the Río Grande and the eventual conversion of the Tejas Indians of east Texas.

1680

Pueblos led by Popé, a medicine man, overthrew the Spanish in Santa Fe. The Pueblo Revolt forced the evacuation of Spanish missions and ranches in the lower Río Grande. Not until 1692, with an expedition led by Don Diego de Vargas, did the Spanish return to Santa Fe in an action called the Reconquest.

1683–84

When the Jumanos asked Governor Antonio de Otermín for aid against the Apaches, he referred the matter to his successor before leaving his office at El Paso. After the Jumanos told of the great kingdom of the Tejas, close neighbors of the Indians of Quivira, new governor Domingo Jironza Petriz de Cruzate prepared an expedition for exploration beyond the Pecos River.

Captain Juan Domínguez de Mendoza and Fray Nicolás López led the expedition as far as present San Angelo, Texas. The explorers killed four thousand buffalo in the vicinity of the Colorado River of Texas, baptized many Indians, and received messengers from several of the east Texas tribes. On the expedition's return to El Paso, its leaders journeyed to Mexico City and recommended the occupation of Jumano country, listing the advantages offered by the "kingdom of Gran Quivira."

1686–93

The French presence in the region expanded during this period, culminating in an attempt to establish a colony at Matagorda Bay under René-Robert Cavalier, sieur de La Salle, in lower Louisiana. Capt. Alonso de León conducted various expeditions beyond the Río Grande into eastern Texas in search of La Salle's colony. Because missions were considered too costly to maintain and because the French at Matagorda Bay had died or scattered, eastern Texas was abandoned in 1693. The Spanish now turned to the central Plains, as it appeared that the French threatened the New Mexico colony from the north.

1696–1706

Following the Reconquest of New Mexico by Don Diego de Vargas in 1692, the Pueblo Indians revolted in 1696. When Governor Vargas led an expedition to Picurís Pueblo, he found it abandoned. On 26 October 1696, Vargas caught up with the fugitives and captured some eighty men, women, and children. The others escaped in the company of Apaches, Tewas, and Tanos. These Picurís Indians were made slaves of the Cuartelejo Apaches.

In 1706 Captain Juan de Ulibarrí led forty soldiers and some one hundred Pueblo auxiliaries to the Plains. Ulibarrí was to ransom the Picurís from their captors and investigate rumors of a French presence reported by friendly Apaches as early as 1695. The expedition left from Taos, apparently crossed Raton Pass, and continued north to the Arkansas River and as far east as the present eastern border of Colorado. After crossing the Arkansas River and reaching the *rancherías* of the Cuartelejo Apaches, they liberated the Picurís Indians without difficulty. They were also told that some seven days' distance from their settlements were the Pawnees, now armed with guns given them by the French.

On his way to liberate the Indians of Picurís, Ulibarrí reported meeting Jicarilla Apache bands and others, called Flechas de Palo, Carlanas, and Penxayes. The Cuartelejo Apaches were farmers and grew corn, pumpkins, beans, and watermelons. They also had French guns and French goods. One of these guns had been taken from a bald Frenchman they had killed after being attacked on the Plains by Pawnees and Frenchmen some days before Ulibarrí's arrival at the central ranchería of El Cuartelejo.

1716

In response to the renewed interest in Texas on the part of the French, Capt. Domingo Ramón led a party of some twenty-five soldiers, forty settlers, eight Franciscan priests, and three lay brothers into East Texas. The mission they founded would eventually become the town of Nacogdoches.

1718

Don Martín de Alarcón, the governor of Coahuila, was appointed governor and captain-general of Texas. He was instructed to establish a way station between the Río Grande outposts and eastern Texas. The expedition, numbering seventy persons, laid the foundations of the presidio of San Antonio de Béjar. The mission of San Antonio de Valero, later known as the Alamo, was founded by Fray Antonio de San Buenaventura Olivares. In 1731 the municipality of San Fernando de Béjar was added to the presidio-mission complex; the civilian settlement initially consisted of ten families of Canary Islanders.

1719

To stop Ute and Comanche livestock raids, New Mexico Governor Antonio Valverde y Cossío decided to punish these Indians. He left Taos Pueblo with some one hundred Spaniards and more than six hundred Pueblo and Apache auxiliaries for the Arkansas River. The Comanches and Utes eluded Valverde, but he learned from the Cuartelejo Apaches that French traders had established two settlements on the South Platte and had formed alliances with the Pawnees, Tejas, and Kansa Indians. Because France and Spain were at war, the news was alarming.

1720

An expedition of forty soldiers, some civilians, and sixty Pueblo Indians led by Don Pedro de Villasur left for the South Platte (Río de Jesús María) to determine whether the French had become military allies of the Pawnees and to investigate the danger to New Mexico should this be true. After being joined by Jicarilla, Carlana, and Cuartelejo Apaches, the expedition was surprised by Pawnees and Otos at the confluence of the Platte and Loup rivers. In a dawn attack, thirty-two Spaniards, including Villasur, and eleven Pueblos were killed. The survivors of the expedition returned to Santa Fe and insisted that Frenchmen were present among the Pawnees in the battle, although their claim remains unproven. Moreover, the site of the battle has been debated. In any case, Villasur's defeat ended the possibility of permanent Spanish expansion onto the Plains north of New Mexico. It was also at this time that the Comanches prevented the French and their allies from moving westward into Spanish territory.

1720

Father Magil de Jesus founded the Mission of San José at San Migel de Aguayo in the San José Valley along the San Antonio River of Texas.

1759

Colonel Diego Ortiz Parilla led an army of over six hundred men (including Spaniards, Mission Indians, Indians from Mexico, and Apaches) from San Antonio against the Comanches and other Plains Indians who had been attacking Spanish mission outposts. Guided by Lipan Apaches, Parilla and his men were led to a Caddoan village near the Red River of Texas. Here the expedition killed fifty-five Indians. The party continued on to Tawehash, a fortified Caddoan and Comanche village. Attempts to storm the village failed, and Parilla and his men were forced to retreat to San Antonio.

1760–1821

The Spanish cautiously consolidated presidios, ranching communities, and missions on the southern Plains of New Mexico and Texas and seldom ventured north.

Selected Bibliography

Bolton, Herbert Eugene, ed. *Spanish Exploration in the Southwest, 1542–1706.* New York: Barnes & Noble, Inc., 1908.

Brandon, William. *Quivira: Europeans in the Region of the Santa Fe Trail, 1540–1820.* Athens: Ohio University Press, 1990.

Brebner, John Bartlet. *The Explorers of North America, 1492–1806.* Cleveland: The World Publishing Company, 1964.

Gibson, Charles. *Spain in America*. New York: Harper Colophon Books, 1966.

Hodge, Frederick W., and Theodore H. Lewis, eds. *Spanish Explorers in the Southern United States, 1528–1543*. New York: Barnes & Noble, Inc., 1965.

Hyde, George E. *Indians of the High Plains: From the Prehistoric Period to the Coming of Europeans*. Norman: University of Oklahoma Press, 1959.

Lowery, Woodbury. *The Spanish Settlements Within the Present Limits of the United States, 1513–1561*. New York: G. P. Putnam's Sons, 1911.

Natella, Arthur A., Jr. *The Spanish in America, 1513–1974: A Chronology & Fact Book*. Dobbs Ferry: Oceana Publications, Inc., 1975.

Sauer, Carl Ortwin. *Sixteenth Century North America: The Land and the People as Seen by the Europeans*. Berkeley: University of Carlifornia Press, 1971.

Webb, Walter Prescott. *The Great Plains*. New York: Grosset & Dunlap, 1931.

Spanish Exploration: Myth

Spanish exploration of the Great Plains did not occur in a knowledge vacuum. It was a part of a worldwide phenomenon emanating from Renaissance Europe. However, because Spanish ideas of human history and the world outside of Europe were based on ancient and medieval texts and the Bible, the Spaniard's conceptualization about exploration and the Plains were based more on myth than on reality. As Ralph H. Vigil relates in the following essay, West became East, and the trinity of motives for Spanish exploration — glory, god, and gold — supported the mythology. Early Spanish explorers to North and South America believed the myths and acted accordingly. Christopher Columbus, Ponce de León, and Francisco Vásquez de Coronado each sought a version of the mythical earthly paradise; Coronado's quest on the Plains was the identification of the Seven Cities of Gold and the land of Quivira.

Vigil connects the myths that motivated Coronado to the driving forces of early Spanish exploration. He traces the myth of the Seven Cities of Gold to the legends of King Roderic of eighth-century Spain, the Pánfilo de Narváez expedition report, and the narrative of Alvar Núñez Cabeza de Vaca. "Fantasies acted as a motivating force for discovery," writes Vigil of Coronado, but instead of finding gold and achieving glory, Spain's son came upon a land rich in architecture, turquoise, and buffalo, the "gold" of Great Plains residents.

The failure of Coronado to realize the myth ushered in the reality of planned settlement and Christian assimilation of the Plains' native peoples. The lack of precious minerals shifted the focus to colonization and trade. Later expeditions took military and surveillance factors into consideration. Still, anchoring the reality of exploration required a redefinition of religious motivations. As Vigil concludes, a European belief in the "primitivism" of native peoples, combined with the millernarian fervor and utopian ideals of the clergy, shaped the Spanish presence on the Great Plains. Religious myths of the world's beginning and end found a receptive audience among sixteenth-century Plains Spaniards.

The following chapter, by Waldo R. Wedel, reveals the difficulty of reconstructing the reality of Spanish exploration on the Great Plains. An archaeologist of long-standing renown, Wedel admires Coronado, a man who "had what it takes." Even so, this ambitious and driven adventurer found no wealth on the Great Plains. The Seven Cities of Gold were mud pueblos; he distrusted his main Indian guide; and his travels across the Staked Plains, the canyons of the Texas Panhandle, and the Arkansas River country brought his expeditionary force great hardship. Although Coronado failed in his desire to make the myth a reality, subsequent investigators have added to the myth by making inaccurate determinations of where Coronado found Quivira. The academic mythmakers erroneously placed Quivira one hundred miles south of Santa Fe by overlooking basic evidence, and they allowed a vainglorious monument erector to identify incorrectly the location of Coronado's farthest penetration north.

Wedel, after years of excavation and study, has pinpointed Quivira in central Kansas, in Rice and McPherson counties near the source of the Little Arkansas River. The discovery and analysis of Spanish chain mail is the key to settling the controversy. But, as so often occurs, answers lead to further questions. What does the spread of Spanish material culture throughout Kansas mean? What about Caddoan religion and Quivira? How successful is the meshing of archaeological evidence and historical evidence in the discovery of Quivira? What about the morality of a European force invading the lands of Native Americans, residents for centuries? To what extent does motivation empower exploration? And what role should archaeology and history play in the tracing of the past? As these essays explain, myth and reality are sometimes difficult to separate as we study the Spanish on the Great Plains.

†

3

Spanish Exploration and the Great Plains in the Age of Discovery

Ralph H. Vigil

This chapter places Spanish exploration on the Great Plains within the context of the temper and feelings prevailing within European culture in the first century of the "discovery" of the West.[1] Because many writers view the past too much through the lens of the present, European expansion in the sixteenth century appears to be more modern than it was. In this chapter Spaniards of the early colonial period are regarded as more medieval than modern in outlook. It is also suggested that mythological geography and a mixture of spiritual and worldly motives, considered incompatible in our day, were as important as Renaissance curiosity and technology in European expansion overseas.

Spanish forays into the Great Plains form part of the tradition of European exploration and settlement of new lands in the period variously called the "Age of Discovery," "Age of Reconnaissance," and "Age of Expansion."[2] Between 1492 and 1598, subjects of Castile explored vast regions of the New World by land and sea, conquered the dominions of the Aztecs and the Incas, founded colonies in Florida and New Mexico, began the spiritual conquest of America, and searched for golden kingdoms in North and South America.

Given the romantic nature of tales of exploration, first-person narratives and biographies of daring adventurers appeal to university students. Though traditional accounts retain their authority and popularity,[3] recent works without copious notes also appeal to a wider public that no longer reads the often-reprinted pioneering studies such as William Hickley Prescott's *History of the Conquest of Mexico* (1843), John Boyd Thacher's *Christopher Columbus* (1903–04), or the significant works of the versatile Hubert Howe Bancroft. Because even the best of the new historical sagas emphasize the deeds of Renaissance men of action, however, they break no new ground, and the motives and personalities of the men directing the expansion of European empires seem more modern than they actually were.[4]

Medieval and Mythic Roots of Discovery

The imagined modernity of the Age of Expansion is even more apparent in textbooks on Western civilization and American history. Written for white, primarily Protestant descendants of transplanted Europeans, these didactic surveys give limited attention to Spanish overseas expansion and the Old and New World backgrounds preceding the founding of Jamestown and Plymouth. In addition to distorting or ignoring Native America, these texts give the impression that a handful of Spanish soldiers exploited and inflicted their culture on the Indians.[5]

Although textbook authors give Indians and Spaniards minor background roles in the epic story of the winning of the West beyond the Atlantic, Iberians actually discovered and took possession of the Americas. Most texts join voyages of discovery, beginning with that of Columbus, to events leading from the Renaissance to the Enlightenment. Overseas expansion is thus related to the rise of nation-states and the sixteenth-century "new monarchies," as well as to new modes of expression in art and religion, dynastic and religious rivalries in the contest for empire, new forms of economic and social life, and the advance of geographical knowledge and technology. As the textbooks have it, rulers of the "new monarchies" favored foreign ventures and the merchant class. Reconnaissance, or what may be called the preliminary exploration of the world beyond Europe, was made possible by practical scientific knowledge. Tools used by the explorers on their "stout, handy, and seaworthy" vessels included the mariner's compass, the astrolabe, and a rudimentary quadrant. Shipborne guns gave Europeans naval superiority. Once a colony was founded, the use of horses, dogs, armor, and superior weapons secured the settlement.[6]

Granted, discovery, exploration, and expansion beyond the seas did take place when Europeans began to join theory and practice in a period that increasingly glorified the human and the natural. However, the idea that Renaissance scientific curiosity, worldly ideals, and the growth of individualism fueled the voyages of discovery is only half true. As one better-than-average text correctly observes, "the motives, the knowledge, and the wherewithal for the great discoveries were all essentially medieval." The impulse to probe the lands across the Atlantic was a mixture of mistaken geographical theory; the desire for spices, gold, and precious stones of the fabulous East; and the memory of medieval journeys made by missionaries and merchants to the Mongol Empire.[7]

America was not only a geographical goal to be reached; it was also a concept to be invented. In the beginning there was the West of the imagination. West became East and was thought to be part of the tripartite world made up of Europe, Africa, and Asia. This unknown land, believed by Columbus to lie at the world's end, evoked feelings of wonder and mystery. The composite West was legendary, theological, and imperial and "might be either a place, a direction, an idea, or all three at once." For some, this cardinal direction brought to mind the setting sun of the vanishing day, "the father of reflection and of the mind's meditation." This region of the world, "the natural goal of man's last journey," represented a higher realm, the second life that follows death.[8] Others looking beyond the dark horizon of the sun's descent saw the planet Venus, which is both the evening and the morning star. Pedro de Castañeda, the chronicler of the Coronado expedition, wrote that "the better land" he and his companions sought might perhaps be entered "through the land which the Marquis of the Valley, Don Fernando Cortés, went in search of under the Western star, and which cost him no small sea armament."[9]

Yet the West was not all heavenly. Monsters, which Thomas More tells us "are common enough," lived there. So did sirens, amazons, griffins, giants, and cannibals.[10] But beyond the dangerous waters of the Atlantic and the fierce beasts and people of the islands and mainland were to be found the waters of life and the legendary lands of happiness. There might be found Antillia, the golden apples of the Hesperides, King Solomon's mines, El Dorado, the land of Cockaigne, the Seven Cities of Cíbola, Quivira, the Fountain of Youth, and the Terrestrial Paradise.

Because modern humans, "with an almost Alexandrian virtuosity," identify independent concepts called economics, religion, legend, history, the natural, the supernatural, and so on, reality becomes compartmentalized. The "natural" is distinguished from the "moral," religion from economics, and the world of the spirit from the world of human affairs. They are placed in separate kingdoms that have no vital connections. As a result, most of us would not question the statement that "mariners, explorers, and conquistadors were religious and 'medieval' in justifying their actions, materialistic and 'modern' in their behavior."[11] But contradictions or out-and-out hypocrisy are merely taken as reflections of the social complexities of an age that still related all activities to religion. As late as the sixteenth century, "contrasts which later were to be presented as irreconcilable antitheses appear in it as differences within a larger unity."[12] Unlike social theorists of today, Christian moralists as late as the sixteenth century attempted to make economic self-interest consistent with a religious standard beyond the letter of the law. They also accepted the feudal system, a hierarchic society in which each stratum had different privileges and functions. Wealth was necessary, but people should receive only those temporal blessings necessary to maintain them in their station.

Given the great power of the nobility in Spain, the aristocracy determined the ideology of the age through its representatives. The religious establishment accepted the hierarchical system; economic self-interest divorced from military and religious ideals was condemned, but wealth joined to nobility and civil power was tolerated as one aspect of feudal and patriarchal relations. The quest for gold was considered an honorable motive for expeditions of discovery as part of a trinity of motives: god, glory, and gold.[13]

Christopher Columbus

Christopher Columbus is described by Ramón Iglesias as America's first merchant and travel agent. Today a mythical figure, he clothed his economic interests with a halo of chivalry. After losing his flagship in December 1492, Columbus founded the fortress and garrison of La Navidad in Hispaniola. He trusted in God that on his return from Castile he would find a barrel of gold, obtained by barter, and hoped that those he left on the island would discover gold mines and spices in such quantity that the king and queen, in less than three years, could undertake the conquest of the Holy Sepulchre: "For so I declared to Your Highnesses, that all the gain of this my enterprise should be spent on the conquest of Jerusalem. And Your Highnesses smiled and said that it pleased them, and that without this profit they had that desire." Columbus, who marks the transition from the waning Middle Ages to the world of commercial capitalism, wrote of wealth in terms of present felicity and future salvation. Iglesias quotes Columbus as saying: "Gold is most excellent, for it constitutes treasure, and he who has it does whatever he wants in the world, and its power is such that it rescues souls from Purgatory to the joys of Paradise."[14]

The mythological geography of America begins with Columbus. His idea that "the world is but small" led him to underestimate the circumference of the globe and expand the breadth of the eastern shores of Asia. These miscalculations had in their favor the opinion of Aristotle, by way of Roger Bacon's *Opus Majus* (1264) and Pierre d'Ailly's *Imago Mundi* (1483); the Moslem geographer Alfragan of the late ninth and early tenth centuries; the Books of Esdras; and *The Book of Ser Marco Polo*.[15] Columbus's geographical misconceptions led to his search for the gold and spices of Cipangu, Cathay, and the Malay Peninsula (the Golden Chersonese); when he reached the mouth of the Orinoco on his third voyage in 1498, they also put him in mind of the paradise lost in the East. Because the river made a great freshwater gulf, he correctly assumed that he had reached a continent. But he also believed that the great river had its source in the Terrestrial Paradise: "Holy Scripture makes known that Our Lord made the Earthly Paradise and in it planted the tree of life, and from it issues a fountain from which rises in the world four principal rivers, the Ganges and Euphrates, the Tigris and the Nile."[16]

Columbus's idea of a fountain in Paradise is not mentioned in Genesis, but it is found in a forgery of the late twelfth century attributed to Prester John, thought to be a rich and powerful Christian ruler of the East or Africa. This hoax was used by the plagiarizing author of Sir John Mandeville's *Travels*, written in the 1360s and widely read throughout the fifteenth century. The fountain of Paradise, whose waters gave lasting health and rejuvenation, was later sought by Juan Ponce de León, a companion of Columbus. Gonzalo Fernández de Oviedo, who knew Ponce de León personally, said the *adelantado* chose to believe a fable that "was a very great ridicule told by the Indians, and a greater stupidity on the part of the Spaniards who wasted their time in looking for such a fountain." Still, as Leonardo Olschki concludes, Ponce de León's search sheds light on the temper and feelings prevailing in the Age of Discovery. The search for the water of immortality is also "a symbol of the human effort to break the power of death and fate."[17]

Columbus and Ponce de León died believing they had reached the shores of farthest Asia. Later explorers, including the chronicler of the Coronado expedition, persisted in this belief. Pedro de Castañeda wrote in about 1562 that New Spain was part of Greater India or China, "there not being any strait between to separate them." He thought the Pueblo Indians of Cíbola had come from "Greater India, the coast of which lies to the west of this country."[18]

Neither Eden's garden nor its fountain was found, but the search for legendary kingdoms and a passage to India continued. Spanish adventurers in search of golden cities sang or recited lines from popular ballads celebrating the heroic deeds of the *reconquista*, and many were avid readers of the novels of chivalry. Dreams of grandeur clouded their minds, and fact was frequently confused with fiction. These hard and austere men were visionaries who gambled temporal life for love of adventure and hopes of glory and gain.[19]

Earthly fame and heavenly glory were harmonized in the idea of spreading the Gospel, gaining great wealth, and winning a good lineage. Most conquistadors failed to achieve renown and prosperity, but sometimes the real and the unreal met in the quest for riches. Bernal Díaz del Castillo's history relates that when the soldiers led by Cortés saw the great cities and towns of the Aztecs "and that straight, level causeway leading into Mexico City, we were amazed and we said that it was like the enchanted things related in the book of Amadis because of the huge towers, temples, and buildings rising from the water, and all of masonry. And some of the soldiers even asked whether the things we saw were not a dream."[20]

Search for the Northwest Passage

North of Mexico, the search for the Fountain of Youth was replaced by the search for the transcontinental Strait of Anián and mythical lands of wealth. This search began with Lucas Vázquez de Ayllón, a royal judge of the Audiencia of Santo Domingo, who was lured to his death by his Indian servant Francisco, captured in the land of Chicora of the pearls. Following the 1517 expedition to Florida of a pilot named Miruelo and another by Alonso Álvarez de Pineda in 1519, Ayllón and other rich men of Cuba sent two ships north in 1521. On this expedition the ships visited lands located between 35 and 37 degrees north latitude. On their return to Santo Domingo, the explorers sighted Chesapeake Bay. Ayllón and his partners thought that the bay might be the mouth of the Northwest Passage sought by Pineda in 1519. Their avarice was fired by the tales of Ayllón's Indian servant, who had been captured near the bay. The Indian, christened Francisco de Chicora, was taken to Spain, where he told Peter Martyr that in the lands visited by Ayllón's ships, there were white men (European fishermen perhaps) with brown hair that hung to their heels. These people possessed domesticated deer and prized pearls and other precious stones, and they were ruled by a man of gigantic size named Datha.[21]

In 1523 the Council of the Indies contracted with Ayllón to find and settle the land ruled by giant King Datha. He was to sail eight hundred leagues inland and was authorized to barter for gold, silver, precious stones, silk, and pearls. However, Ayllón, who delayed his expedition until 1526, learned in 1525 that the pilot Estevan Gómez (who deserted Magellan in the straits to the south) had sailed from Florida to Newfoundland but had not found a strait to Cathay. Ayllón now changed his expedition of discovery to one of colonization and trade. He left for the north with five hundred men, eighty or ninety horses, and a great quantity of trade goods. On the voyage the flagship and all supplies were lost, no pearls or other wealth were found, and Francisco de Chicora and other Indian interpreters escaped. After the settlement was founded (perhaps in Virginia) Ayllón died on 18 October 1526, "when there followed divisions and murders among the chief personages, in quarrels as to who should command." Only 150 sick and starving men returned to Hispaniola and Puerto Rico.[22]

Not all of Francisco de Chicora's tales were products of the imagination. Thirteen years after Ayllón's death, Hernando de Soto landed in Florida, turned his back to the sea, and went in search of the province of Cofitachequi. There, in the sepulchers of the dead, Soto found eight or nine *arrobas* of pearls, a dirk, green beads, rosaries with their crosses, and the iron axes brought to that land by Ayllón. Many of the pearls, "worth their weight in gold," had lost their hue because their holes had been bored with heat. At the town of Talomeco, a league distant from Cofitachequi, a great store of pearls was found in a temple more than a hundred feet in length and forty in width. However, many had been damaged by being buried in the earth and covered with the fat of dead Indians. Close to the portals of the temple were images of twelve fierce giants, "carved in wood and copied from life."When the Spaniards showed the beautiful *cacica* of Cofitachequi rings of gold and silver coins as examples of the metals they desired, her subjects brought Soto "a great quantity of very golden and resplendent copper" and "great iron pyrites which were as thick as boards." No silk was found, but mulberry trees formed part of the grove surrounding Cofitachequi.[23]

Legends and Tales of the Seven Cities

At about the same time that Soto was exploring and robbing graves in the great area known as Florida, Juan Rodríguez Cabrillo was mapping the coastline north of Mexico, and Francisco Vázquez de Coronado was chasing down rumors of mythical Indian cities of great wealth in New Mexico and the Great Plains of present-day Kansas and western Texas. Coronado's search for the Seven Cities of Gold and the fabulous land of Quivira has its origins in a medieval legend, tales told to Nuño Beltrán de Guzmán (president of the first Audiencia of Mexico), and the voyage of Pánfilo de Narváez to Florida in 1528. Hence, although Plains exploration in the eighteenth century was primarily for military or surveillance purposes, expeditions north from Mexico led by Agustín Rodríguez and Francisco Chamuscado (1581), Antonio de Espejo (1582–83), Gaspar Castaño de Sosa (1590), and Francisco Leyva de Bonilla and Antonio Gutiérrez de Humaña (1593) were inspired by dreams of wealth, the idea of spiritual conquest, or a combination of both motives.

A legend of the late Middle Ages related that when King Roderic lost Spain to the Arabs in 711, the archbishop of Porto and six other bishops sailed westward with many people for the island of Antillia. There they built seven cities, and so that their subjects might not think of returning to the mainland, they burned their ships.[24] This legend of seven fabulous cities in the West merged with a story told to Nuño Beltrán de Guzmán by an Indian slave in 1530. The Indian, called Tejo by the Spaniards, told Guzmán that as a boy he and his father had visited seven very large towns rich in gold and silver. These towns were named "The Seven Cities" and were thought to be some

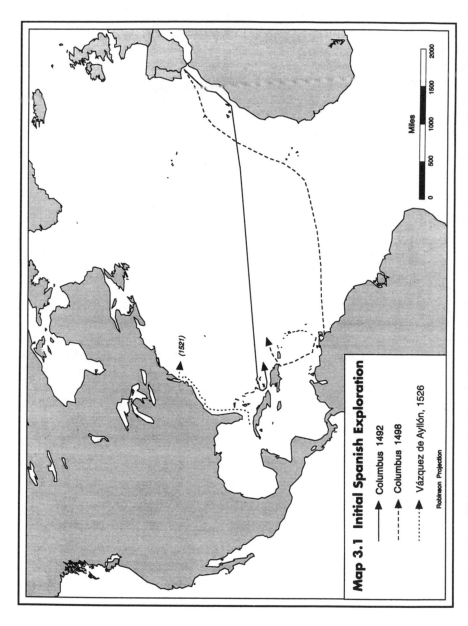

Initial Spanish Exploration.

forty days' distance to the north of Michoacán.[25] Six years later, Alvar Núñez Cabeza de Vaca, Andrés Dorantes de Carranza, Alonso de Castillo Maldonado, and Estevan, the blackamoor slave of Dorantes, arrived on the northern frontier of New Galicia. Their tale of adventure reinforced the idea of "another Mexico" beyond the northern horizon.

The four castaways, the only survivors of the expedition to Florida led by the inept Pánfilo de Narváez in 1528, made a report of their remarkable overland journey to Viceroy Antonio de Mendoza. Cabeza de Vaca, Dorantes, and Alonso de Castillo also drew up a report in Mexico City for the Audiencia of Santo Domingo. This joint report and the more famous narrative of Cabeza de Vaca, first printed in 1542, related that the wanderers had heard from the Sonora Indians that there were very populous towns to the north with very large houses whose inhabitants possessed fine turquoises.[26]

The rainbow seekers had also seen "clear traces of gold and lead, iron, copper, and other metals," and Cabeza de Vaca had been given five emeralds made into arrowheads by Indians. The idea of converting the Indians of the north to Christianity and of finding great wealth caused the viceroy to chase down these rumors. Meanwhile, Fray Antonio de Ciudad Rodrigo, the Franciscan provincial, sent three friars on ships commissioned by Don Fernando Cortés to make a voyage of discovery in the South Sea (Pacific Ocean). This expedition of 1538 "arrived in Cíbola, a thickly populated land similar to Spain which extends as far as Florida."[27]

Coronado's Search for the Seven Cities

In the same year, Fray Antonio sent Fray Marcos de Niza and the lay brother Onorato to the north by way of the Pacific coast. They formed part of an expedition led by Francisco Vázquez de Coronado in search of new lands. When the friars and Coronado found two roads in the land of Topira north of Culiacán, Coronado elected to explore the road to the east, and the friars took the road to the west. After a few days, the group led by Coronado reached rugged sierras and decided to return to San Miguel de Culiacán. Meanwhile, Onorato fell ill, but Fray Marcos, in the company of the black slave Estevan and another interpreter, followed the road that led to the coast. Fray Marcos came to a land inhabited by a poor people, who treated him well. From them he learned of a thickly populated land farther north whose people had houses of two and three stories in enclosed towns on the shore of a great river. Beyond the river were larger towns, and the land was rich in turquoise and buffalo.[28]

The legend of the Seven Cities of Gold was superimposed on the tales told by the Indians, and Fray Marcos de Niza's second expedition to the north in 1539 appeared to confirm the cities' existence. Estevan was sent ahead of the main party and reached the Zuñi settlements before Fray Marcos. At Zuñi Estevan offended the Indians by requesting turquoise and women. The Indians also thought it unreasonable for him to say that "the people were white in the country from which he came and that he was sent by them, he being black." Taken for "a spy or a guide from some nations who wished to come and conquer them," Estevan was killed by the inhabitants of Zuñi, but the Sonora Indians who accompanied him "were allowed to return freely to their own country."[29]

When Fray Marcos, sixty leagues from Cíbola, heard of Estevan's death, he claimed to have gone forward and seen Cíbola, a city of fine appearance larger than the seat of the viceroyalty, with stone houses, terraces, and flat roofs. This lie, or what may have been an optical illusion, persuaded the viceroy in 1540 to send Coronado north at the head of three hundred Spaniards and some eight hundred Indians. Fray Marcos went along as father provincial. When the Spaniards arrived at Hawikuh, the first of the seven "cities" of the Zuñi, they cursed Fray Marcos: It was nothing more than "a little crowded village" that looked "as if it had been crumpled all up together." Castañeda listed seventy-one villages of Pueblo Indians, agricultural communities having little wealth, with some twenty thousand men and a total population of perhaps eighty thousand.[30]

Coronado's Search for Quivira

At Zuñi, the Spaniards were welcomed by a delegation of Indians from Pecos (Cicuye). The party that went to Pecos returned to the Tiguex pueblos on the Río Grande, where Coronado chose winter quarters. The returning delegation brought an Indian slave of the buffalo plains who had served at Pecos. This Indian, called the Turk, claimed that Quivira lay to the east of his country. In addition to having much gold and silver, this version of El Dorado featured fish as big as horses in a river two leagues wide (perhaps catfish on the Mississippi). The Turk claimed that on the river there were

> large numbers of very big canoes, with more than twenty rowers on a side, and that they carried sails, and that their lords sat on the poop under awnings, and on the prow they had a great golden eagle. He said also that the lord of that country took his afternoon nap under a great tree on which were hung a great number of little gold bells, which put him to sleep as they swung in the air. Everyone in that land had his "ordinary dishes made of wrought plate, and the jugs and bowls were of gold."[31]

When the Río Grande thawed out in the spring of 1541, the army left the vicinity of the future Albuquerque to search for Quivira on the eastern plains. After crossing the river and the mountains, the seekers entered the Great Plains. Past the Pecos River, near the present eastern boundary of New Mexico, they met the eastern Apaches (Querechos). These "intelligent" people conversed so well by means of sign language, the lingua franca of the Plains, "that there was no need of an interpreter." After reaching the Canadian River, the Turk led the army southeast to the Staked Plains. According to Coronado, this flat country covered by grama and buffalo grass was "as bare of landmarks as if we were surrounded by the sea. Here the guides lost their bearings because there is nowhere a stone, hill, tree, bush, or anything of the sort. There are many excellent pastures with fine grass."[32]

The Texas (Tejas) Indians, a Caddoan-speaking people who guided the Spaniards, were kind and faithful friends who hunted the buffalo. Castañeda described buffalo hair as wool that "ought to make good cloth because of its fineness." The buffalo bulls had bulging eyes, very long beards (like goats'), and short tails "with a bunch of hair at the end. When they run, they carry it erect like a scorpion." The plentiful white wolves of the Plains hunted the buffalo cows. In their march to Quivira under a vast expanse of sky, the Spaniards also saw rabbits, kidney beans and prunes, groves of mulberry trees, walnuts, and rose bushes like those of France.

After marching 250 leagues from the Tiguex villages on the Río Grande, Coronado realized that he had been deceived by the Turk. His captains and ensigns agreed that Coronado "should go in search of Quivira with thirty horsemen and half a dozen foot soldiers," and the rest of the army should go back to Tiguex.[33] Using Texas Indians as guides, Coronado reached Quivira after traveling either forty-two or forty-eight days. He was received peacefully by the Wichita Indians in the vicinity of present-day Great Bend, Kansas. The people of Quivira lived in grass lodges, and their lord "wore a copper plate on his neck and prized it highly." When no gold or silver was found, Coronado had the Turk garroted. After he rejoined the army at Tiguex, the soldiers endured the winter "almost naked and poorly clothed, full of lice, which they were unable to get rid of or avoid."[34] Coronado promised the soldiers that they would again search for Quivira, but he fell from a horse during a race, and in April 1542, still not fully recovered, he announced the army would return to New Spain.

Many of the soldiers, encouraged by Fray Juan de Padilla, wanted to continue the search for Quivira, but the general's orders pleased a good number of the explorers. Because they "did not stumble over bars of gold and silver immediately upon commencing their march into these regions, and because the streams and lakes and springs they met flowed crystalline waters instead of liquid golden victuals, they cursed the barren land and cried out bitterly against those who had led them into such a wilderness."[35]

More Searches to the North

Coronado's failure to find gold and silver did not dispel the idea that vast wealth was to be found in the north. Five years after the disillusioned Coronado returned to New Spain, "there was official talk of sending new expeditions to colonize Quivira," and the plan to Christianize the north began immediately.[36] Fray Juan de Padilla, obsessed by the Seven Cities, elected to return to Quivira, but he was soon killed by Indians there. However, the utopian dream of the spiritual conquest of northern New Spain, including lands visited by Coronado and Soto, continued to inspire the Franciscan order of New Spain. In 1558, a decade after the silver mines of Zacatecas revealed the mineral wealth of northern Mexico, Alonso de Zorita, royal judge of the Audiencia of Mexico, and Fray Jacinto de San Francisco, a lay brother of the Franciscan order, were encouraged by Franciscan missionaries and Fray Bartolomé de Las Casas to propose "an expedition numbering approximately 100 soldiers and 20 Franciscans into the Land of War beyond Culiacán and Chichimeca territory. The region to be entered led to Florida, New Mexico, Copala, lands discovered by Coronado, and other fertile provinces inhabited by large populations ripe for conversion and potentially rich in gold and silver mines." This plan confirmed the idea of many Spaniards of Mexico that the happiness of the province would be assured by the conquest of the land of Florida, "which one can reach quickly and easily by sea, and the way is not too difficult by land."[37]

The Council of the Indies found the plan proposed by Fray Jacinto and Zorita fanciful and excessive, and no expedition was sent out. However, the concept did have a certain significance and result. In addition to being "the first of many joint endeavors on behalf of the Indians during the next few years" by Bartolomé de Las Casas and the Mexican missionaries, the plan may have resulted in the peaceful settlement of the region beyond Zacatecas in the 1560s. Moreover, when the policy of "war by fire and blood" failed to win northern Mexico, new approaches emerged that closely resembled the proposal of Zorita and the Franciscans.[38] Spanish domination of northern Mexico was finally achieved "by a combination of diplomacy, purchase, and religious conversion." Food and clothing were given to the natives, and prospective Indian farmers were promised good land, seed, and agricultural implements. Concludes Philip Wayne Powell, "Out of the experience of this pacification grew the mission system that was to serve Spain so well in her expansion on the American continent."[39]

The work of conversion by the regular orders on "the rim of Christendom" led to a greater knowledge of the native civilizations of northern Mexico, the Río Grande Valley, and the Great Plains. In many instances, this knowledge was interpreted as reinforcing conventions found in Renaissance thought and literature: the "noble savage," the Golden Age of simplicity, and the Garden of Eden before the fall.

In the same way that Old World tales of fantastic and marvelous El Dorados obtruded between the Spaniards and America's reality, the idea of Paradise or the Golden Age of antiquity led to primitivism, the idea that Indians lived in harmony with nature and reason, free from measures, money, and greed. As Peter Martyr observed shortly after Columbus's first voyage to the Indies, the Indians lived "in a golden age, without laws, without lying judges, without books, satisfied with their life, and in no wise solicitous for the future." Drawing on this imagery, Pedro de Castañeda observed that the Pueblo Indians lived in peaceful simplicity. Ruled by a council of the oldest men and guided by their priests, these communal people worked together to build their villages. Their virgins went nude, in the manner of Eve before the

Fall. Before marriage "the young men served the whole village in general, and only after taking a husband did the women cover themselves." The Pueblo people were exceptionally clean and kept separate houses for the preparation of food. While a man played the fife, the women sang and ground grain to the music.[40]

The Spanish linked millennialism to primitivism in articulating the role of the mission system of New Spain. Critical of the corruption of Europe and its deviation from "natural law," friars and humanists looked backward to an Indian Golden Age in which people lived happily and simply. They also looked forward to a Christian utopia that would redeem the tragic lives of the Indians who had fallen under Spanish rule. Millennialism and primitivism were the opposite sides of a single coin, and the missionaries hoped to create an Indian terrestrial paradise consecrated to poverty and knowledge of the true God.[41]

Conclusion

Gold and conversion symbolized America in the sixteenth century, and those who would win them would be covered with glory. America was a European dream that gradually faded and became transformed into new myths and new realities. America became America, but it was first conceived as Asia and was measured by medieval Christian and classical traditions. Classical geography, Judeo-Christian and Greco-Roman traditions, and Old World myth, fable, and fiction accounted for the initial invention of America. Reality gradually impinged, but as late as 1598 José de Acosta noted that Spaniards still remained ignorant of the lands between Peru and Brazil. Some said it was an inundated land, full of lakes and marshes; others said it had great and glorious kingdoms and imagined the Paytiti, El Dorado, and the Land of the Caesars, where there were marvelous things.[42]

Explorations in this period have an essential unity in their mythic quality and religious thematic elements. Exploration on the Great Plains cannot be understood if separated from the Spanish search for the Terrestrial Paradise, El Dorado, King Solomon's mines, and other great and glorious kingdoms. As America became better known, legendary kingdoms kept moving farther and farther west; the Spanish search for King Solomon's mines eventually led to the discovery of the great circle route to Mexico from the Philippines.[43]

In this instance and others, fantasy acted as a motivating force for discovery. Ideas and legends of medieval origin became a part of the history of America: California takes its name from a mythical island "at the right hand of the Indies" ruled by Queen Calafía and her Amazons and rich in gold and griffins. Myth continues to influence the American mentality and helps determine the shape of reality and the country's future. The smoke of dreams envelops the form of the actual for good and evil. Today, America the Beautiful has become the Mecca of the Miraculous, and we look to the myth of star wars technology to preserve the myth of the land of the free and the agrarian utopia of the Plains.[44]

Notes

1. The elusive West can be either the entire Western Hemisphere or various New World frontiers where westward-moving Europeans or their descendants confronted *"in their own territory* the original possessors of the continent." For a definition of the mythological West and the"Western" as a type of adventure literature, see Leslie Fiedler; *The Return of the Vanishing American* (New York: Stein and Day, 1976), pp. 16–49, and Robert F. Berkhofer, Jr., *The White Man's Indian* (New York: Vintage Books, 1979), pp. 96–104. For those who subscribe to the frontier thesis of U.S. history, there are successive "Wests." The frontier, "a migrating geographic area," is "the meeting point of savagery and civilization, the zone where civilization entered the wilderness" (Ray Allen Billington, *Westward Expansion: A History of the American Frontier* [New York: The Macmillan Company, 1967], pp. 1–11).

2. Arthur Percival Newton, ed., *The Great Age of Discovery* (London: University of London Press, 1932); J. H. Parry, *The Age of Reconnaissance: Discovery, Exploration and Settlement, 1450 to 1650* (New York: Praeger Publishers, 1969); Charles E. Nowell, *The Great Discoveries and the First Colonial Empires* (Ithaca: Cornell University Press, 1954).

3. George Parker Winship's translation of Pedro de Castañeda's narrative of the Coronado expedition has been reprinted without scholarly apparatus several times. See Winship, "The Coronado Expedition, 1540–1542," in *Fourteenth Annual Report of the Bureau of Ethnology to the Secretary of the Smithsonian Institution, 1892–1893*, Part 1 (Washington, D.C.: Government Printing Office, 1896). There are several translations of the journey of Alvar Núñez Cabeza de Vaca. See "The Narrative of Alvar Núñez Cabeza de Vaca," in Frederick W. Hodge and Theodore H. Lewis, eds.,

Spanish Explorers in the Southern United States (1907; rpt. New York: Barnes & Noble, 1946), pp. 1-26; Fanny Bandelier, trans. and ed., *The Journey of Alvar Núñez Cabeza de Vaca and His Companions from Florida to the Pacific, 1528–1536* (New York: A. S. Barnes & Co., 1905); and Cyclone Covey, trans. and ed., *Cabeza de Vaca's Adventures in the Unknown Interior of America* (1961; rpt. Albuquerque: University of New Mexico Press, 1983). Other explorers' narratives are found in the Hakluyt Society's *Works* and Cortes Society's *Documents and Narratives*. For major trends in the writings by U.S. scholars on colonial Spanish America, see Benjamin Keen, "Main Currents in United States Writings on Colonial Spanish America, 1884-1984," *Hispanic American Historical Review* 65 (1985): 657-82. See also Ralph H. Vigil, "Exploration and Conquest," in E. R. Stoddard, R. L. Nostrand, and J. P. West, eds., *Borderlands Sourcebook: A Guide to the Literature on Northern Mexico and the American Southwest* (Norman: University of Oklahoma Press, 1983), pp. 31-35.

4.   See Samuel E. Morison's *Admiral of the Ocean Sea: A Life of the Admiral Christopher Columbus*, 2 vols. (Boston: Little, Brown, and Company, 1942). Rewritten for a wider public in 1954 and titled *Christopher Columbus, Mariner*, it appeared as a Mentor book. This work is traditional and conservative; the author states, "My main concern is with the Columbus of action . . . I am content to leave his 'psychology,' his 'motivation' and all that to others" (1942, p.6). The most durable general work on Spanish discovery, exploration, and conquest is Edward Gaylord Bourne's *Spain in America, 1450–1580*, first published in 1904. Bourne's sympathetic interpretation of Spain's Indian policy was influenced by the climate of opinion that made for U.S. expansionism and the creation of an overseas empire between 1865 and 1914. For a criticism of the "bardic version of the Columbian voyages and their consequences" by "narrative historians, most of them nineteenth-century writers" who described "the American past in ways consonant both with the documentary record then available and with the ethnocentrism of their fellow white citizens of the New World, particularly of the United States," see Alfred W. Crosby, Jr., "The Columbian Voyages, the Columbian Exchange, and Their Historians," in Michael Adas, ed., *Essays on Global and Comparative History* (Washington, D.C.: American Historical Association, 1987), pp. 1-29.

5.   For the treatment of Indians in educational texts, see James Axtell, "Europeans, Indians, and the Age of Discovery in American History Textbooks," *American Historical Review* 92 (June 1987): 621-32; Frederick E. Hoxie, "Teaching History Today," *Perspectives* 23 (April 1985): 18-22; and Neal Salisbury, "Indians in Colonial History," (Chicago: D'Arcy McNickle Center for the History of the American Indian, Occasional Papers in Curriculum, Washington Conference, 1985), No. 4, pp. 1-26.

   As Axtell notes, American college students are "still being shown the Spanish empire through the distorting lens of the 'Black Legend.'" One popular college textbook claims that "only selected persons" migrated to the New World and that these few were male and exploitative. We are also told that Spanish colonists quickly mated with Indian and black women, "thereby creating the racially mixed population that characterizes Latin America to the present day" (Mary Beth Norton et al., *A People and a Nation: A History of the United States*, 2 vols. [Boston: Houghton Mifflin Company, 1986], 1:16). This text also claims that Spain failed to establish true colonies, i.e., *agriculturally based* settlements inhabited by literate, white men and *women* who read and understood the King James version of the Bible (p. 20).

Norton et al. state that "approximately two hundred thousand ordinary men and women" (p. 20) came to North America in the seventeenth century. Although the authors view these early colonists as very religious people, they fail to note Jon Butler's point that "American colonists had an ambivalent relationship with Christian congregations" and that the English colonists "proved surprisingly ignorant of elemental Christian beliefs" (Jon Butler, "Magic, Astrology, and the Early American Religious Heritage, 1600-1760," *American Historical Review* 54 [April 1979]: 317-46). They also fail to mention that emigration from Spain to the New World in the years 1492-1600 may have reached 200,000 or more. Perhaps 450,000 Spanish emigrants came to the New World in the seventeenth century. At the end of the sixteenth century, 35.3 percent of the emigrants to the Indies were women. See articles by Woodrow Borah, Peter Boyd-Bowman, Magnus Mörner, and James Lockhart in Fredi Chiappelli et al., eds., *First Images of America: The Impact of the New World on the Old*, 2 vols. (Berkeley: University of California Press, 1976), 2:707-804. Although legally forbidden to migrate to the Indies, converted Jews and Moors and the hopeless, the bankrupt, the criminal, and the delinquent of Spain were found in the Indies in abundant numbers. By 1550 the *conversos* of Hispaniola controlled the island politically and economically. See Ralph H. Vigil, *Alonso de Zorita: Royal Judge and Christian Humanist, 1512–1585* (Norman: University of Oklahoma Press, 1987), pp. 41-82.

Racial and cultural mixture between Spaniards and other ethnic groups is usually considered to have taken place in the New World colonies, giving rise to the idea that *pure* Spanish blood was diluted by Indians and blacks. This ignores the fact that Spaniards had experienced ethnic and "racial" *mestizaje* before their arrival in America. As Brian R. Hamnett notes in his review of Philip Wayne Powell's *Tree of Hate: Propaganda and Prejudices Affecting United States Relations with the Hispanic World*, "Much more needs to be said about the racial and cultural *mestizaje* within Spain before the American expansion. Here, precisely, may lie the *real* root of foreigners' contempt for Spaniards. The great flowering of sixteenth- and early seventeenth-century Spain should not be viewed in our future research without references to this medieval past. Similarly, *mestizaje*, always subject to denigration, is the most interesting, significant, and enduring contribution of Latin America to a world poisoned by deeply rooted racism" (*Hispanic American Historical Review* 53 [1973]:

671-72). For discussions of *mestizaje* in Spain, see Vigil, *Alonso de Zorita*, pp. 44-45, 246, 248; Magnus Mörner, *Race Mixture in the History of Latin America* (Boston: Little, Brown and Company, 1967), p. 16; and Claudio Esteva Fabregat, *El mestizaje en Iberoamérica* (Madrid: Editorial Alhambra, 1988), pp. 127-28. For the different kinds of Spaniards who came to the Indies, see J. Vicens Vives, ed., *Historia de España y América*, 5 vols. (Barcelona: Editorial Vicens-Vives, 1961) 3; 393-97. At the end of the colonial period there may have been 3.2 million "whites" in Spanish America. Lucas Alamán stated that 1.2 million Spaniards resided in New Spain; of these, 70,000 were *peninsulares* (Lucas Alamán, *Historia de México*, 5 vols. [México: Editorial Jus, 1942] 1: 17, 30).

6. For the tools of the explorers, see J. H. Parry, *Europe and a Wider World* (London: Hutchison University Press, 1966), pp. 13-25. For the idea that Spain under the Catholic Kings was not the "new monarchy" theoretically characteristic of the renaissance state, see J. H. Elliott, *Imperial Spain, 1469-1716* (New York: New American Library, 1977), pp. 75-76.

7. Edward McNall Burns et al., *Western Civilizations: Their History and Their Culture* (New York: W. W. Norton, 1984), pp. 457–59; see also Edward P. Cheyney, *The Dawn of a New Era, 1250–1453* (New York: Harper Torchbooks, 1962), pp. 276-97.

8. Loren Baritz, "The Idea of the West," *American Historical Review* 66 (April 1961): 618-40, quoted pp. 619, 620; Hartley Burr Alexander, *The World's Rim* (Lincoln: University of Nebraska Press, 1967), p. 17.

9. Hodge and Lewis, *Spanish Explorers in the Southern United States*, p. 283. For Venus as a symbol of purity and evil, see Joseph Campbell, *The Hero with a Thousand Faces* (Princeton: Princeton University Press, 1968), p. 303; see also Old Testament, Isaiah, 14: 12–15.

10. Thomas More, *Utopia*, ed. Edward Surtz (New Haven: Yale University Press, 1964), p. 14. More had read Amerigo Vespucci's account of his voyages, which mentions giants, cannibals, and Indians who lived 150 years. On his first voyage Columbus looked for human monsters; he found none but did have a report of an island called "Caniba" by some Indians, and by others "Carib." This island was supposed to be inhabited by a ferocious people "who eat human flesh." On 8 January 1493, Columbus "saw three sirens, who rose very high from the sea, but they were not as beautiful as they are depicted for somehow their faces had the appearance of a man." The Indians at Samaná Bay also told him that the island of Matinino (Martinique) was "entirely peopled by women without men" (Christopher Columbus, *The Journal of Christopher Columbus*, trans. Cecil Jane, ed. L. A. Vigneras [London: Hakluyt Society, 1960], pp. 143, 146-47, 200). For the idea that griffins had lived in Mexico's great sierras and in the Río de La Plata region and Peru, see Alonso de Zorita, *Historia de la Nueva España*, ed. Manuel Serrano y Sanz (Madrid: Imprenta de Fortanet,

1909), pp. 222-24. Zorita also noted that the Indians related things that appeared to be fables, stating that giants had arrived in Mexico by way of the Pacific Ocean. "In order to feed each one of these giants, it was necessary for one hundred Indians to grind corn for tortillas. They were thus assigned various regions in the land so that they might be fed, and their bones have also been found in Peru and in the East Indies and in some parts of Spain." The Indians of Mexico also told Zorita that "in ancient times bearded and very tall men had arrived in the land; this surprised them because they have the custom of shaving their beards" (pp. 224-26).

11. Julio Caro Baroja, *The World of the Witches*, trans. O.N.V. Glendinning (Chicago: University of Chicago Press, 1973), p. 9; R. H. Tawney, *Religion and the Rise of Capitalism* (New York: Mentor, 1954), pp. 11-60; John P. McKay et al., *A History of Western Society*, 2 vols. (Boston: Houghton Mifflin, 1983) 1: 519.

12. Tawney, *Religion and the Rise of Capitalism*, p. 25.

13. Mariano Picón-Salas, *A Cultural History of Spanish America from Conquest to Independence*, trans. Irving A. Leonard (Berkeley: University of California Press, 1971), pp. 34-35.

14. Ramón Iglesias, *El hombre Colón y otros ensayos* (México: El Colegio de México, 1944), pp. 17-49, quoted p. 49; Bartolomé de Las Casas, *Historia de las Indias*, ed. Agustín Millares Carlo, 3 vols. (México: Fondo de Cultura Económica, 1951) 1: 282-83.

15. Boies Penrose, *Travel and Discovery in the Renaissance, 1420-1620* (Cambridge: Harvard University Press, 1952), pp. 8-9; Ferdinand Columbus, *The Life of the Admiral Christopher Columbus,* trans. and ed. Benjamin Keen (New Brunswick: Rutgers University Press, 1959), p. 16; George E. Nunn, *The Geographical Conceptions of Columbus* (New York: American Geographical Society). See also A. P. Newton, "Introduction: The Conception of the World in the Middle Ages," in A. P. Newton, ed., *Travel and Travellers of the Middle Ages* (New York: Barnes and Noble, 1926), pp. 1–18.

16. Nunn, *Geographical Conceptions of Columbus*, pp. 70-75; Las Casas, *Historia* 2: 43. Columbus believed the earthly paradise would be found far inland where earth was closest to heaven. He believed that the Western Hemisphere (which began 100 leagues beyond the Azores) was pear-shaped and had a high projection like a woman's nipple on a round ball. As a result, ships rose gently toward the sky beyond the Azores and the weather became milder. He noted that the people he found at Trinidad and the mainland were whiter (or less dark) than Africans living in the

same latitude. Moreover, the fairer people he met at Trinidad and the mainland lived in milder temperatures, their hair was long and smooth, and they were of greater intelligence and not cowardly (Las Casas, *Historia* 2: 41; Cecil Jane, ed., *Select Documents Illustrating the Four Voyages of Columbus* [London: Hakluyt Society, 1933], pp. 32-36).

17. Leonardo Olschki, "Ponce de León's Fountain of Youth: History of a Geographic Myth," *Hispanic American Historical Review* 21 (May 1941): 361-85; Malcolm Letts, ed., *Mandeville's Travels: Texts and Translations*, 2 vols. (London: Hakluyt Society, 1953) 1:121-22, 2: 325-26, 376, 459-60. Prester John's letter stated that in the wood situated at the foot of Mt. Olympus (Ceylon) there "springs a clear fountain which has within itself every kind of taste. It changes its taste every hour by day and night, and is scarcely three days' journey from Paradise, whence Adam was expelled. . . . [He] who tastes of this fountain thrice, fasting, will suffer no infirmity thereafter, but remains as if of the age of 32 years as long as he lives." Mandeville wrote that the terrestrial paradise "is the highest land of the world, and it is so high that it touches near the circle of the moon" (Letts, *Mandeville's Travels* 2:505, 1:215–16). Columbus, like Mandeville, understood that "no man living may go to Paradise." By land, says Mandeville, the way is blocked by wild beasts and impassable hills and rocks. "By water also may no man pass thither, for those rivers come with so great a course and so great a birr and waves that no ship may go ne sail against them." In summary, Mandeville and Columbus placed Eden's garden "so far in the east that it is also at the extremist end of the west" (Newton, *Travel and Travellers*, p. 164). See also George Boas, *Essays on Primitivism and Related Ideas in the Middle Ages* (Baltimore: Johns Hopkins Press, 1948), pp. 154-74; Gonzalo Fernández de Oviedo, *Historia general y natural de las Indias*, 5 vols. (Madrid: Biblioteca de Autores Españoles, 1959) 2:102. As Campbell observes (*Hero with a Thousand Faces*, pp. 172–92), the desire for physical immortality is as old as the epic of Gilgamesh and as modern as George Bernard Shaw's *Back to Methuselah*.

18. Winship, "The Coronado Expedition," pp. 447, 454, 513, 525.

19. Ramón Menéndez Pidal, *The Spaniards in Their History*, trans. Walter Starkie (New York: W. W. Norton, 1966), p. 20; Antonio Pastor, "Spanish Civilization in the Great Age of Discovery," in Newton, *Great Age of Discovery*, pp. 10-44; Federico Fernández de Castillejo, *La Ilusión en la Conquista* (Buenos Aires: Editorial Atalaya, 1945), pp. 13-17.

20. Bernal Díaz del Castillo, *The Discovery and Conquest of Mexico, 1517–1521*, trans. A. P. Maudslay (New York: Grove Press, 1956), pp. 190-91, quoted in Irving A. Leonard, *Books of the Brave* (New York: Gordian Press, 1964), p. 43.

21. Francis Augustus MacNutt, *De Orbe Novo: The Eight Decades of Peter Martyr D'Anghera* (New York: G. P. Putnam's Sons, 1912), pp. 259, 267-65.

22. Manuel Lucena Salmoral, "La extraña capitulación de Ayllón para el poblamiento de la actual Virginia: 1523," *Revista de Historia de América*, nos. 77-78 (January–December 1974), pp. 9-31; Oviedo, *Historia general*, 4: 327; Hodge and Lewis, *Spanish Explorers*, p. 174.

23. Oviedo, *Historia general*, p. 168; Garcilaso de la Vega, El Inca, *The Florida of the Inca*, trans. and ed. J. G. Varner and J. J. Varner (Austin: University of Texas Press, 1951), pp. 303–16. The weight of the pearls found varies depending on the report consulted. The factor (business manager) of the expedition, Luis Hernández de Biedma, stated that about seven *arrobas* were found (an *arroba* is equivalent to 25 pounds). Another member of the expedition, the Gentleman of Elvas, states that 350 pounds of pearls were found. It thus appears that the Inca Garcilaso de la Vega exaggerates when he writes that "there were more than 1,000 *arrobas* of pearls and seed pearls." See Inca Garcilaso de la Vega, *La Florida del Inca: Historia del Adelantado Hernando de Soto, Gobernador y Capitán General del Reino de la Florida, y de otros heroicos caballeros españoles e indios* (México: Fondo de Cultura Económica, 1956), p. 220. See also Hodge and Lewis, *Spanish Explorers*, p. 174.

24. Enrique de Gandia, *Historia crítica de los mitos de la conquista americana* (Madrid: J. Roldán y compañía, 1929), pp. 59-69. The island of Antillia, or the Island of the Seven Cities, described as some 2,500 miles from Japan and 200 leagues due west of the Canaries in the 1470s, was allegedly visited by a Portuguese ship in the time of Prince Henry the Navigator (1394-1460). When the sailors visited the church of Antillia, "the ship's boys gathered sand for the firebox and found it was one-third fine gold." Other ships of Portugal sought Antillia in the years before Columbus's discovery but could not find it. Following the discovery, the island of Hispaniola was called Antillia by the Portuguese; Amerigo Vespucci called it Antiglia. See F. Columbus, *The Life of the Admiral*, pp. 21, 25-27; Las Casas, *Historia* 1: 64, 68; 2: 119, 161, 212; and Angélico Chávez, O.F.M., *Coronado's Friars* (Washington, D.C.: Academy of American Franciscan History, 1968), pp. 15-16.

25. Hodge and Lewis, *Spanish Explorers*, pp. 285-87.

26. Oviedo, *Historia general*, 4: 311.

27. Hodge and Lewis, *Spanish Explorers*, pp. 106, 111; Alonso de Zorita, "Relación de las cosas notables de la Nueva España y de la conquista y pacificación della y de la doctrina y conversión de los naturales," Biblioteca del Real Palacio, Madrid, MS 59 (1585), folio 496. For interpretations of the

route of the castaways, see Donald E. Chipman, "In Search of Cabeza de Vaca's Route Across Texas: An Historiographical Survey," *Southwestern Historical Quarterly* 91 (October 1987): 127-145.

28. Zorita, "Relación," folios 496-97; Fray Toribio de Motolinia, *Historia de los indios de la Nueva España* (Barcelona: Herederos de Juan Gili, Editores, 1914), pp. 173-75; Francis Borgia Steck, trans., *Motolinía's History of the Indians of New Spain* (Washington, D.C.. Academy of American Franciscan History, 1951). Aside from Zorita and Motolinia (Fray Toribio de Bonavente), no chroniclers or documentary sources that I have found mention Fray Marcos's making a journey north in 1538. What is certain is that the instructions for the 1539 expedition given to Fray Marcos were accepted by him on 20 November 1538. As early as 15 July 1539, Coronado wrote the king that Fray Marcos, accompanied by native Indians and the Negro Estevan, had traveled into the interior of the country beyond Culiacán and had discovered "a very fine country" (George P. Hammond and Agapito Rey, trans. and eds., *Narratives of the Coronado Expedition, 1540–1542* [Albuquerque: Coronado Cuarto Centennial Publications, 1940], pp. 45–49, 61, 63–82).

29. Hodge and Lewis, *Spanish Explorers,* pp. 289-90. Fray Marcos's report does not agree with Castañeda's narrative. The friar wrote that two of the Indians who escaped told him that of the Indians who accompanied Estevan to Cíbola, "more than three hundred were dead" (Hammond and Rey, *Narratives of the Coronado Expedition,* p. 76).

30. Hammond and Rey, *Narratives of the Coronado Expedition,* p. 79; Chávez, *Coronado's Friars,* p. 12; Hodge and Lewis, *Spanish Explorers,* pp. 300, 358-59.

31. Hodge and Lewis, *Spanish Explorers,* p. 314.

32. Ibid., p. 330; Hammond and Rey, *Narratives of the Coronado Expedition,* p. 186. In his study of the Llano Estacado, or the Staked Plains, William B. Conroy notes that the landscape through which the Spaniards passed "and the forms of life they encountered, including the buffalo and the Plains Indian, were described with accuracy and in detail" ("The Llano Estacado in 1541: Spanish Perceptions of a Distinctive Physical Setting," in Oakah L. Jones, Jr., *The Spanish Borderlands — A First Reader* [Los Angeles: Lorrin L. Morrison, 1974], pp. 24-32; originally published in *Journal of the West* [October 1972]).

33. Hodge and Lewis, *Spanish Explorers,* pp. 335, 382-83.

34. Ibid., pp. 336, 337, 367; Hammond and Rey, *Narratives of the Coronado Expedition,* p. 187.

35. Chávez, *Coronado's Friars*, p. 58; Gaspar Pérez de Villagra, *History of New Mexico*, trans. Gilberto Espinosa (Los Angeles: The Quivira Society, 1933), pp. 58-59.

36. Herbert Eugene Bolton, *Coronado, Knight of Pueblos and Plains* (Albuquerque: University of New Mexico Press, 1940), p. 400. As late as 1720 the governor of Coahuila, the Marquis of San Miguel de Aguayo, led five hundred mounted troops into eastern Texas to check French defenses beyond the Red River and to discover Quivira. See Luis Weckmann, *La herencia medieval de México*, 2 vols. (México: Colegio de México, Centro de Estudios Históricos, 1984) 1: 63.

37. Vigil, *Alonso de Zorita*, p. 218, quotation p. 217.

38. Alonso de Zorita, *Life and Labor in Ancient Mexico: The Brief and Summary Relation of the Lords of New Spain*, trans. Benjamin Keen (New Brunswick: Rutgers University Press, 1963), p. 50; Henry Raup Wagner with Helen Rand Parish, *The Life and Writings of Bartolomé de Las Casas* (Albuquerque: University of New Mexico Press, 1967), p. 231.

39. Philip Wayne Powell, *Soldiers, Indians and Silver: The Northward Advance of New Spain, 1550–1600* (Berkeley: University of California Press, 1952), p. 204.

40. MacNutt, *De Orbe Novo*, pp. 79, 103-04; Hodge and Lewis, *Spanish Explorers*, pp. 352-54.

41. For primitivism and millennialism and their relationship to the Golden Age of simplicity and the Garden of Eden where "no pleasing habit ends," see Berkhofer, *The White Man's Indian*, pp. 72-75; see also Mircea Eliade, *Myths, Dreams and Mysteries* (New York, Harper, 1960), pp. 39-43; Hoxie Neale Fairchild, *The Noble Savage: A Study in Romantic Naturalism* (New York, Columbia University Press, 1928), pp. 1-22; and Henri Baudet, *Paradise on Earth* (New Haven: Yale University Press, 1965). For the Franciscan belief that they had been "given the unique opportunity of creating, on the eve of the world, a terrestrial paradise where a whole race of men would be consecrated to evangelical poverty," see John Leddy Phelan, *The Millennial Kingdom of the Franciscans in the New World* (Berkeley: University of California Press, 1970).

42. José de Acosta, *The Natural and Moral History of the Indies* (London: Hakluyt Society, 1880), p. 171. Acosta also noted that "some affirm there is another strait under the North, opposite to that of Magellan," and that "the new world, which we call Indies, is not altogether severed and disjoined from the other world . . . I have long believed that the one and the other world are joined and continued one with the other in some part, or at the least are very near" (pp. 18, 60).

43. Harry Kelsey, "Finding the Way Home: Spanish Exploration of the Round-trip Route Across the Pacific Ocean," *Western Historical Quarterly* 17 (April 1986): 145-64.

44. The name "California" probably comes from a novel of chivalry called *Las Sergas de Esplandián*, written by Garcí Rodríguez de Montalvo and published in Saragoza in 1508, in Seville in 1511, in Rome in 1519, and in many subsequent editions. It was translated into French, Italian, English, German, Dutch, and Hebrew and forms part of the series of the Amadis de Gaula novels of chivalry. For Amazons and Calafía's islands, see Leonard, *Books of the Brave*, pp. 36-53; for the American West as symbol and myth in the imagination of nineteenth-century America, see Henry Nash Smith, *Virgin Land: The American West as Symbol and Myth* (Cambridge: Harvard University Press, 1950).

✝

4
Coronado and Quivira

Waldo R. Wedel

Slightly more than 450 years ago, the Kansas prairies were visited for the first time by white men. These were a select group of Spanish adventurers from Mexico led by a thirty-year-old nobleman by the name of Francisco Vázquez de Coronado. Francisco was a lad of eleven years when Hernán Cortés conquered the Aztec capital of Tenochtitlán, now Mexico City, and sent back to Spain a vast treasure in gold, silver, and precious stones. One of several younger sons, and thus denied by the rule of primogeniture from inheriting any significant share of the family patrimony, Francisco followed the example of many of his contemporaries and headed for the land of promise — the New World. He arrived in Mexico City with the viceroy, Antonio de Mendoza, a year or two after Francisco Pizarro, a cousin of Cortés, plundered the Inca capital of Cuzco in Peru, greatly enriching himself and returning another fabulous fortune to Spain. Within two years of his coming, Don Francisco married a beautiful, wealthy, and well-connected heiress. By 1538, three years after his arrival in Mexico, Coronado, still only twenty-eight years old, was appointed to the governorship of New Galicia on the northwestern frontier of New Spain. The record strongly suggests that Coronado had what it takes.[1]

Coronado's Expedition

Along with the sixteenth-century treasure seekers and soul savers from Spain, there came to the New World rumors of the legendary Seven Cities, a long-lived and widely traveled European tradition. An interesting constellation of circumstances eventually located these

tered two or three days' march downstream from the crossing. Three or four days later, on about 6 July, the Spaniards came to their village.

Locating Quivira

Despite some very good clues in the Coronado documents, the identification of the Quivira sought by the Spaniards has been a subject of lively discussion for well over a century. It has been located in many places — in New Mexico, Texas, Oklahoma, Kansas, Colorado, Missouri, Nebraska, South Dakota, and even across the Missouri River in Iowa. Many of these identifications rest on an amazing disregard of the information that can be ferreted out of the Coronado documents — the distances and directions reportedly traveled, the number of days spent, the terrain traversed, and other details. One group of mid-nineteenth-century writers argued that the ruins of Quivira were less than a hundred miles south of Santa Fe. Why seventy-seven days were required for such a relatively short trip was not explained. Before Herbert E. Bolton did so in 1940, no one had troubled to retrace the route of the conquistadors from Compostela to Quivira on the ground. Writers worked instead with maps and drew mainly on personal familiarity with certain segments of the route, leaving further correlations and integration for the future.

The better informed and more competent scholars of the late nineteenth century, such as H. H. Bancroft, A. F. Bandelier, George P. Winship, and Frederick Webb Hodge, had settled on a Kansas location as the most likely.[3] Of these men, Hodge came closest when he argued that the first settlements of Quivira reported by Coronado were only a short distance east of the city of Great Bend, Kansas.[4] By 1900 Johan August Udden, a young Swedish-born instructor at Bethany Academy in Lindsborg, Kansas, had witnessed the unearthing of a piece of chain mail in an Indian trash mound on Paint Creek in McPherson County. In a scholarly report that earned him high praise in a review by Hodge, Udden suggested the possibility of a visit from the Spaniards into the region.[5]

Udden's report of the chain mail was followed in 1902 by Minnesotan Jacob V. Brower's decision to have monuments erected to record "for all time the discovery of Quivira by Coronado in 1541 and its rediscovery in 1896 by Brower."[6] The energetic and highly motivated Brower erected a Minnesota granite shaft in Logan Grove, Kansas, two miles south of Junction City in Geary County, and placed smaller ones in three adjoining county seats that he said were also the site of Quivira — Alma, Wabaunsee County; Manhattan, Riley County; and Herington, Dickinson County.[7] It was a good try and not more than a hundred miles wide of the mark.

Digging in Central Kansas: A Personal Reflection

Shortly after my arrival at the U.S. National Museum (Smithsonian Institution) in mid-August 1936, I was instructed to set up a research program in archaeology in an area of my own choosing. The result was a four-year project aimed at reexamining the scattered, often promising, but generally unintegrated fieldwork and diggings that had been carried on at various times in Kansas. Central Kansas — the Quivira problem — was set for attention in 1940, the fourth summer. This would be the four-hundredth anniversary of Coronado's departure from Mexico; it was also the summer in which Bolton was retracing the route of the Spanish march from Mexico to Quivira.[8]

In Lyons, Kansas, meanwhile, the search for Quivira had been under way since 1927. In that year, Paul and Horace Jones, the owners and operators of the *Lyons Daily News*, had staged a "mystery window" night with the Lyons Commercial Club. When the *Daily News* window was unveiled, it featured the Jones' collection of Indian artifacts, which had been found on various farms in the Lyons area. Thereafter, Indian relics from this locality, looked upon as the remains of Quivira, began accumulating and kept alive the steadily growing interest in local antiquities.

With one assistant, I arrived in Lyons on the Smithsonian field party in early June 1940. We contacted Horace Jones at the *Lyons Daily News* and then tried unsuccessfully to acquire digging privileges at the Tobias and C. F. Thompson sites some eight miles north and east of the city. The next morning, armed with a letter of introduction from Jones, we secured permission from Mr. and Mrs. John Malone to work on their land, most of which was in cultivation, four miles west of Lyons. Cache pit depressions and two larger basins that we thought might be house sites were visible in a small piece of unbroken prairie pasture. Mrs. Malone strongly believed that Indian burial grounds, which abounded on her farm, should not be disturbed. Accordingly, she stipulated that we could not dig in more than two mounds and could only excavate a short trench along the fence line, where no crops would be damaged. As no mounds were visible, we persuaded her that we should be allowed to open two cache pits without disturbing more than ten square feet of pasture around each pit. Our trench was to be not more than thirty feet long by three feet wide. And, of course, all the earth that was removed would be replaced on completion of our tests.

Before starting to dig, and in hopes of doing better elsewhere, we proceeded to Lindsborg and sought permission to dig at Paint Creek or at nearby Sharps Creek. Sharps Creek was unavailable because the owner's son was planning to continue digging there himself and outsiders were not welcome, even as nonworking observers. At Paint Creek, where Udden had worked intermittently from 1881 to 1888, Ed Nelson was willing to let us dig, but only after harvest a week or ten days hence. So back we went to Rice County to set up camp near Buffalo Bill's well on the Malone property. It was not a very rewarding dig, but we were greatly impressed when Malone's son, who was cultivating the adjoining field, called our attention to potsherds, worked flints, ash, charcoal, and quantities of animal bones being turned up at many points by his plow. Cache pits were evidently present by the score, but Mrs. Malone remained adamant, and we could only look across the fence and wonder what we were missing.

Three days after we began operations at the Malone site, Horace Jones came out with word that he had gotten us permission to dig at the Tobias site. He also said he had written C. F. Thompson in Indiana for approval of limited testing of the Thompson site across the Little Arkansas River, whose permanent flow originated less than half a mile upstream. These permissions were forthcoming, and our Rice County program for the summer was assured. Later we moved south to Cowley County to work at the Arkansas City Country Club and other nearby sites that were closely related to the Rice County site. This is the area to which I now think Juan de Oñate came in 1601. Much of the 1940 work has been reported in detail.[9]

After that first summer, thanks in considerable part to Horace Jones and the *Lyons Daily News*, doors began to open to us everywhere in Rice County. The *Daily News* carried a story about the dig every day. We came back in 1965, 1966, and 1971. We were granted access and excavation privileges at sites we were warned would be forever closed to us because the owner intended to work them himself. We opened cache-trash pits, trenched rubbish heaps, tested three "council circles," and searched with little success for lodge sites and house floors.

Since 1940 it has been my conviction that the Quivira visited by Coronado in 1541 lay generally between the Smoky Hill River and the big bend of the Arkansas River, extending eastward to include the Walnut River and the headwaters of the Cottonwood River around Marion and west to include Barton County. In all probability, many more sites remain to be recorded, both within the geographical limits here suggested and beyond them.

Prior to the beginning of intensive agriculture, these sites were marked by low mounds, on and in which there was plentiful evidence of past human domestic activity, including a good many artifacts of stone, bone, shell, and pottery. Long regarded as house ruins, the mounds are now known to mark one-time trash heaps. Scattered among the middens are innumerable erstwhile storage pits last used as garbage dumps. Some of these measure up to eight feet deep, are of equal diameter, and can be entered only with a stepladder; their capacity may be calculated at one hundred to two hundred bushels. From these have been taken quantities of broken pottery and numerous lost and discarded stone objects, worked and unworked animal and bird bone, charred corn, beans, sunflower seeds, and a wide range of other items. There is some evidence, too, of former shallow house floors fifteen to twenty inches deep and perhaps twenty-five to thirty feet in diameter. The Wichita Indians, who were probably the natives visited by Coronado and other early European explorers, were reported to be living in grass-covered houses of this general type and size.[10]

At three sites in Rice County and two in McPherson County, there are, or formerly were, large ditched circles with mounded centers. No site has more than one such circle, and not all sites have one. These enigmatic forms have long been known as "council circles" locally, but this term is used without any real basis and has no grounding in ethnohistory.[11] At least two of the ditches are elliptical rather than circular. From one of these circles were taken several charred ears of choice seed corn that had evidently been stored within a shallow coiled basketry tray; freshwater mussel shells found nearby contained small quantities of red ochre. Another circle yielded a necklace of pale blue pea-sized glass trade beads separated by bird-bone spacers, with turquoise beads and a pendant at the lower end.[12] Still another produced

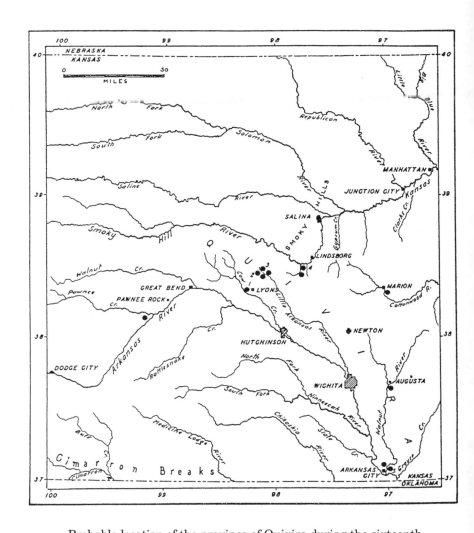

Probable location of the province of Quivira during the sixteenth and seventeenth centuries. Solid circles indicate sites visited or partially excavated by the U.S. National Museum in 1940. Numbers indicate the following sites: 1. Malone site; 2. Tobias site; 3. Thompson site; 4. Udden site; 5. Arkansas City Country Club site. Courtesy of the Smithsonian Institution.

an iron ax head.[13] Well-made red stone pipes were taken from several of the basins in which these materials were recovered. Otherwise the artifact inventory from the basins and the caches in them paralleled that taken from trash pits elsewhere in the sites.

The three council circles in which we made subsurface tests must, I think, be regarded as special-purpose structures, perhaps men's lodges or their equivalent. Each had a large central fireplace. Our investigations have provided at least a partial answer to the riddle of the circles: On 21-22 December 1965, two groups of local observers stationed themselves at my suggestion on a line connecting the Hayes and Thompson council circles and verified the alignment of the circles with the winter solstice sunrise horizon points.[14]

The fourscore interested observers who were present and looking west from the Hayes council circle on 22 June 1978 at summer solstice time will recall how the sun, two or three minutes before setting, slipped out from behind a thick cloud bank and then dipped beneath the horizon dead center between the Thompson and Tobias circles. This was exactly where Dr. John A. Eddy of the High Altitude Observatory in Boulder, Colorado, also present, had predicted it would set. That was, I think, the most dramatic moment in our five seasons of work in Rice County.

In addition to turning up Indian artifacts of local manufacture, which can be found in other central Kansas sites, excavation at the Quivira sites has yielded imported objects. Especially noteworthy are the glaze-paint decorated potsherds that recur again and again.[15] Originating among the Pueblo Indians of the Río Grande Valley and the Galisteo Basin, these include the following named potterywares: Pojoaque polychrome, Tewa polychrome, Kotyiti glaze polychrome, Puaray glaze polychrome, and Espinosa glaze polychrome.[16] Most of these belong to the glaze-paint wares that date from the early fifteenth to the middle eighteenth centuries and thus bracket the period of intensive Spanish exploration and expansion in the Great Plains. They provide a most helpful means of cross-dating between the Pueblo and Plains Indian areas.

Of no less interest are the rare items of metal and glass that have come to light in the central Kansas sites. They are far less common

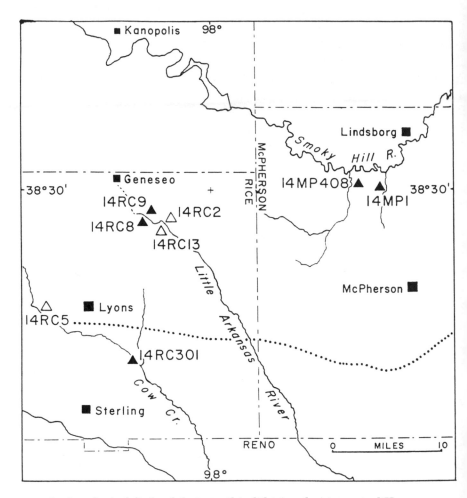

Archaeological finds of chain mail (solid triangles) in central Kansas.
Dotted line is Santa Fe Trail route. Courtesy of the
Smithsonian Institution.

than are the products of local Indian manufacture and suggest that
European traders had not yet become established among these Indians. The pieces have all been found within twenty miles of the later
Santa Fe Trail, which may well have followed an old Indian trail used
by native trader-entrepreneurs for decades.

Chain Mail in Kansas

Of particular interest are the fragments of chain mail that have been found in undisturbed context in no fewer than six sites.[17] The first piece was found on the Paint Creek site (14MP1) between 1881 and 1889 by Udden.[18] Lost for many decades, it was acquired some years ago by the Kansas State Historical Society. At Paint Creek, two collectors from Salina found additional bits of mail identified by Randolph Bullock, curator of arms and armor at the Metropolitan Museum of Art in New York. A badly rusted mass and several free rings were found at the C. F. Thompson site (14RC9), and these were examined by Stephen V. Grancsay, also of the Metropolitan. A member of my 1971 field party found another small mass at the Tobias site (14RC8) near the floor of an eighty-one-inch deep cache pit. Two large masses that are possibly from separate garnments were found near the bottoms of two cache pits mostly destroyed by floods of Cow Creek at the Saxman site (14RC301),[19] and sample rings were examined by Grancsay and his Metropolitan colleague Helmut Nickel.[20] Another specimen was excavated recently at the Majors site (14RC2). In addition to Grancsay, Bullock, and Nickel, Harold Peterson of the National Park Service examined most of these specimens at my request and judged that there was nothing inconsistent with the view that all were from the general Coronado period, although their precise date and place of manufacture cannot be ascertained.[21]

Chain mail is a flexible fabric of interlaced metal links. It is designed for protection against piercing weapons — arrows, darts, spears, and the like. It is much better ventilated and thus more comfortable than the plate armor that eventually superseded it in general use. Its popularity peaked in Europe in the tenth to thirteenth centuries, a period sometimes called the "Age of Mail."[22] By 1600, mail was declining in popularity in western Europe, though its manufacture was never discontinued entirely. Explorers and adventurers from western Europe found mail garments satisfactory in their encounters abroad with lightly armed native peoples during the golden half century of Spanish and Portuguese exploration from 1492 to 1542.[23] Mail was also worn by horses. According to Peterson, "the Spanish who made the long treks with De Vaca, Coronado, and De Soto, and who founded the first permanent settlements in Florida, were the most heavily armored group ever to come to America."[24]

Mail shirt said to have belonged to Aleksandr Baranov, ca. 1800.
Open at sides and bottom. Light-colored portions are stainless steel
restorations. Photo courtesy of the Smithsonian Institution
(USNM 237848).

The methods of manufacturing chain mail varied from place to place and from time to time.[25] Again according to Peterson, the usual process during the period of early Spanish exploration

> was to wind a wire tightly about an iron rod and then cut it off in rings. The ends of each ring were then flattened and punched for a rivet. Garments were constructed from these rings by linking them together and then riveting the individual rings. Occasionally, European mail is found in which the ends of alternating rows of rings were welded instead of riveted, but the latter were more common. Normally, each ring was linked with four others. An ordinary shirt of mail would weigh from 14 to 30 pounds (6.5 to 13.5 kgs.) depending upon the size of the rings and the overall size of the garment.[26]

Flat or half-round stock was commonly used after the invention of drawn wire but was superseded by round wire after the sixteenth century. Unfortunately, neither the date nor place of manufacture can be established for individual pieces when they do not bear a maker's tag. Most rings in the Kansas pieces are about eight to eleven millimeters in diameter and include both half-round and round stock and riveted and unriveted links.

To the best of my knowledge, archaeological finds of chain mail in the Great Plains have been made only in Kansas. They have been found in context with a native material culture complex associated with the sixteenth and seventeenth centuries and thus are apparently contemporary with early Spanish explorations northward from Mexico. No chain mail has yet turned up in Pawnee sites in Nebraska, nor in Oklahoma, Colorado, Missouri, or elsewhere on the Great Plains.[27]

Attempts to pinpoint the source of the chain mail garments and fragments found in central Kansas revolve around the Coronado *entrada* of 1541. The expedition's muster roll, which includes the names of most participants and identifies the sort of equipment they were carrying, suggests some support for the possibility. For example, in the troop of "230-odd" horsemen there were 552 horses, 56 coats of mail, three pairs of mail leggings, two pairs of mail sleeves, and three loin guards and skirts of mail. Some people took several chain mail garments along. There is no record of any of these being lost during the expedition.[28]

For the next official expedition, that of Juan de Oñate in 1601, we have the inspection record made by Juan de Frías Salazar before the

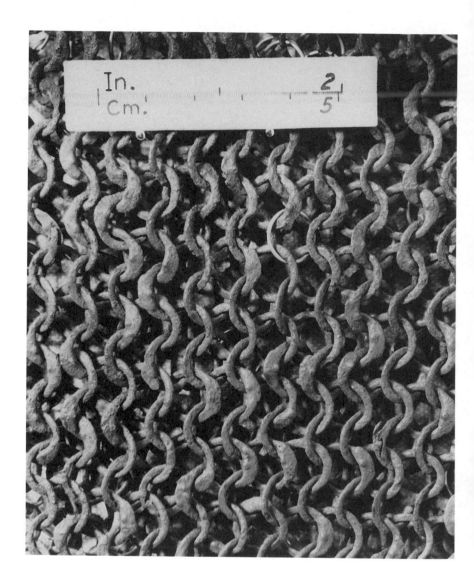

Detail of Baranov mail shirt fabric. Note flattened and widened
segments of links closed by riveting and visible rivet ends. Photo
courtesy of the Smithsonian Institution.

Chain mail fragment (Kansas State Historical Society 74.70) from the
Paint Creek site, 14MP1, McPherson County, Kansas, found between
1881 and 1889. Photo courtesy of the Smithsonian Institution.

Chain mail en bloc (rusted together) from Saxman site, 14RC301,
found in 1974 and now in Rice County Historical Museum, Lyons,
Kansas. Maximum dimension 7.5 inches (19 cm). Photo courtesy
of the Smithsonian Institution.

party left Mexico. A number of participants were provided with coats
of mail. At least twelve men who accompanied Oñate to Quivira
reported one or more pieces, and he himself claimed ten. Vicente de
Zaldívar, Oñate's *maese de campo* on the Quivira trip, had three, "plus
one fine coat of mail." Gaspar López claimed three coats of mail,
including "one of fine quality," plus two cuisses (thigh guards) of
"coarse mail." No record has been found of how many of these pieces
returned to Mexico with the expedition.[29]

Between Coronado's journey in 1541–42 and that of Oñate in
1601, at least one other expedition reached Quivira, and it might well
have been the source of the mail. This was an unauthorized campaign
led by Capt. Francisco Leyba de Bonilla and Antonio Gutiérrez de
Humaña. Apparently no journal survives. The party was eventually

wiped out almost to a man, probably somewhere between the Arkansas and Smoky Hill rivers in Kansas. If this party was equipped and armed along the lines of the Coronado and Oñate expeditions and was essentially destroyed, such arms and metal armor as its members carried were probably divided among the Indians as war trophies.

The Case for Kansas as Quivira

The summer of 1940, when my Rice County investigations for the Smithsonian Institution began, was also the summer in which Herbert C. Bolton completed his fieldwork on Coronado and the Quivira question. Alone among the many who have worked or toyed with these matters, Bolton followed by horse, mule, auto, and foot the route of Coronado's march, with documents in hand. He had done much archival research with unpublished documents in Mexico and in Spain, thus acquiring insights and new information to which his predecessors had no access. He and I missed contact by a few weeks that summer in Lyons, but he wrote me shortly after our fieldwork ended to inquire about the archaeological evidence we had turned up. Ultimately, Bolton accepted Rice and McPherson counties and adjacent central Kansas as the location of Coronado's province of Quivira.[30]

Unlike the majority of those who have traveled this fascinating road before, and armed with archaeological evidence that none of them had, I am persuaded that the location of Coronado's province of Quivira in central Kansas is now firmly established. I am not arguing for the infallibility of archaeology or of archaeologists. I cheerfully concede that no matter how flowery the rhetoric, a researcher bases his or her conclusions on possibly fallible interpretations of imperfect and incomplete data. That said, to the best of my knowledge no other section of the interior United States fits the geographical, historical, and archeological requirements of the Coronado documents as well as Rice and McPherson counties do. Nowhere else on the Plains does Río Grande glaze-paint-decorated pottery datable to the Coronado period recur at site after site. Nowhere else does chain mail occur repeatedly with that pottery and with wares, stone, and bonework of clearly local manufacture, with only limited quantities of European trade or gift materials. To the historian these points are significant because they provide glimpses of a native Indian society uncontaminated by European influences and datable with some degree of precision. They thus form a sound foundation on which to build further research into the past.

Viewing that evidence once again, I hold to the position I reached more than four decades ago[31] — namely, that:

1. the Quivira of the sixteenth- and seventeenth-century Spanish documents and the central Kansas archaeological sites were habitat of one and the same native people;

2. Coronado's 1541 entrada into the province of Quivira in all-likelihood took place in present Rice and McPherson counties; and

3. larger sites such as Malone, Saxman, Tobias, and Paint Creek were very likely among the grass-house villages whose Wich-ita-speaking inhabitants greeted the bearded and travel-worn strangers from the south on that memorable day in early July 1541.

Hodge, Bolton, John R. Swanton (my 1970 colleague), and a few others about whose work I am perhaps less well informed were on the right track. Once these scholars had accepted that the Quivira River (which Coronado had also named "the River of Saints Peter and Paul") was the Arkansas River, they could not easily come to any other conclusion. The Spaniards had crossed this northeast-flowing river six or seven days below Quivira and proceeded downstream along its north bank until they reached their destination. The archaeological evidence that would clinch the case that Quivira was in central Kansas came later, thanks to Paul and Horace Jones, the two self-styled country editors who for more than four decades doggedly utilized the influence of the local press in attracting serious institutional investigations.

Unanswered Questions

By no means have all of the questions about Quivira been answered, not even the major ones. One of the most intriguing puzzles involves an intaglio figure located about one and a half miles south of the Hayes and Tobias council circles atop a prairie bluff, overlooking a small intermittent creek. This figure is of serpentine form, about 160 feet long. At the south end is what might be taken for a curled-up tail;

two faintly marked open jaws at the north end hold between them an oval elevation, suggesting an egg. This intaglio is scarcely six inches deep and is further set apart by a short-grass cover, contrasting sharply with the surrounding mid-grass prairie sod. The acuteness with which this figure can be seen depends rather strongly upon the angle at which the sun strikes it, much like the Great Serpent Mound in Ohio. In a nighttime test several years ago, the open jaws appeared to line up with two council circles — the left one with the Tobias circle and the right one with the Hayes circle. Not all observers have accepted the reality of this intaglio or of its orientation. However, having seen it in short and tall grass and having seen its apparent correlation with two of the three council circles, I am strongly inclined to believe that it was made by the Quiviran natives and, further, that it had some esoteric connection with the council circles.

One wonders, too, whether Friar Juan de Padilla, had he escaped early martyrdom at the hands of unfriendly Indian neighbors of the Quivirans, could have left us further enlightening details regarding the rituals of the people and their special religious observances.

Notes

An earlier version of this paper was read on April 27, 1985, at a symposium for the dedication of the Coronado-Quivira Museum in Lyons, Kansas.

1. See generally Herbert E. Bolton, *Coronado: Knight of Pueblos and Plains* (Albuquerque: University of New Mexico Press, 1940), and Stewart L. Udall, *To the Inland Empire: Coronado and Our Spanish Legacy* (Garden City: Doubleday and Co., Inc., 1987).

2. See Mildred Mott Wedel, "The Indian They Called Turco," in Don G. Wyckoff and Jack L. Hofman, eds., *Pathways to Plains Prehistory*, Memoir 3 [Cross Timbers Heritage Association, Contributions 1] (Norman, OK: Oklahoma Anthropological Society, 1982), pp.153–62.

3. See generally Hubert Howe Bancroft, *History of Arizona and New Mexico, 1530–1888* (San Francisco: The History Company, 1889); Adolph F. Bandelier, *The Gilded Man (El Dorado) and Other Pictures of the Spanish Occupancy of America* (New York: D. Appleton & Co., 1893); George Parker Winship, "The Coronado Expedition, 1540–1542," *Fourteenth*

25. Carlyle Shreeve Smith, "Methods of Making Chain Mail (14th to 18th Centuries)," *Technology and Culture* 1 (1959): 60–67, 289–91.

26. Peterson, *Arms and Armor,* p. 107.

27. But see Bruce T. Ellis, "A Possible Chain Mail Fragment from Pottery Mound," *El Palacio* 62 (1955): 181–84.

28. Arthur Scott Aiton, "Coronado's Muster Roll," *American Historical Review* 44 (Number 3, 1939): 556–70; George P. Hammond and Agapito Rey, *Narratives of the Coronado Expedition* (Albuquerque: University of New Mexico Press, 1940), 2: 87–108.

29. Aiton, "Coronado's Muster Roll"; Hammond and Rey, *Narratives*. See also *Don Juan de Onate, Colonizer of New Mexico, 1595–1628*, Coronado Cuarto Centennial Publications (Albuquerque: University of New Mexico Press, 1953), 5: 228ff.

30. Bolton, *Coronado*, pp. 291–95.

31. See W. Wedel, "Archeological Remains in Central Kansas."

Spanish Settlement: Reality

The Spanish first entered the Great Plains from the south during the sixteenth century. For two hundred years Spain avoided the Llano Estacado, also known as the High Plains or the Staked Plains. This region was perceived by the Spaniards as a transitionary zone, a land to control but not necessarily to settle.

To be sure, exploration penetrated the interior. Coronado reported on the buffalo, Indians, and environmental features of the Llano Estacado. Other expeditions set out in search of gold, such as the Rodríguez–Sánchez Chamuscado expedition of 1580, the Antonio de Espejo expedition of 1581, and Gaspar Castaño de Sosa's expedition in 1590. Settlement was still not a major part of the plan, however.

Félix D. Almaráz, Jr., tells how forbidding the Llano Estacado was to potential emigrants. Early Spaniards recognized the nature of the environment, and some even attempted to accommodate to it. Missionary probes characterized the first half of the seventeenth century, followed by military initiatives for the next century. Good relationships with the native peoples of the southern Plains were extremely important for any kind of permanent settlement. Comanches, Pueblos, Jumanos, Apaches, Tejas, Kiowas, and others entered into diplomatic relations with their new neighbors. And the Spanish were extremely concerned about other Europeans, especially the French.

Almaráz concludes his essay with graphic evidence of how historians have misinterpreted the nature of the Spanish presence on the southern Plains. The fact that settlement was less important to Spain than missionary, military, and diplomatic goals in the region does not indicate any lack of commitment to the region; rather, the region's environment did not welcome large numbers of any group, be they Hispanic, Anglo, or Indian. Not until twentieth-century technology brought underground water to the surface did major migrations come to the southern Plains, and these migrations contained a sizable Latino population.

One of the most prominent Spanish military expeditions of the eighteenth century was the Villasur expedition of 1720. Thomas Chávez examines evidence and lost artifacts to explain both the complexity of the Spanish relationship to the Plains and the difficulty of identifying its history. Specifically, Chávez discusses three paintings

✝

5
An Uninviting Land: El Llano Estacado, 1534–1821

Félix D. Almaráz, Jr.

Throughout the colonial period, Spanish pioneers carefully avoided the plains of present-day western Texas as a potential area of permanent settlement. Essentially because of the absence of dependable water resources, an all-important consideration in the selection of occupation sites,[1] Hispanics generally regarded this territory with respectful awe and apprehension. Spanish law, as prescribed in the *Recopilación de las leyes de los reynos de las Indias,* prohibited settlers, notwithstanding personal initiative and the availability of land in great abundance, from occupying a region that lacked reliable sources of fresh water.[2]

From the sixteenth to the eighteenth centuries, the Spaniards preferred to colonize adjacent areas of the borderlands, such as New Mexico's *río arriba* district or central and eastern Texas. The Plains, including the awesome Llano Estacado, were merely an unimportant imperial claim that explorers and veteran frontiersmen occasionally traversed with utmost caution. The Hispanic presence on the plains of western Texas and eastern New Mexico was thus random and transitory for hundreds of years.[3]

Geography of the Llano Estacado

The plains of modern-day Texas form the southern extension of an even larger physiographic division that stretches north from the Río Grande across the level west into Canada. This expansive province includes several well-defined subdivisions, two of which — the High Plains and the Pecos Lowland — extend from West Texas across into eastern New Mexico. The High Plains region is itself a broad physiographic entity, bounded on the east by the Caprock escarpment, on the west and southwest by the Pecos Lowland, on the southeast by the Edwards Plateau country, and on the north by "the wide and rather deep erosion groove" created by the Canadian River in the Texas Panhandle.[4]

The High Plains constitute one of two prominent geographical components of the region settlers of European descent called the Panhandle. In contrast to the Caprock, an escarpment of hard caliche or chalk crust that extends roughly in a north-south pattern, the West Texas plains then possessed distinctive economic advantages — maximum rainfall use, rich topsoil, and verdant native grasses — that eluded the vision of Spanish travelers intent on other goals.[5] Over the eons, nature had produced on the West Texas plains an area that, according to geologist Nevin M. Fenneman, "is as flat as any land surface" imaginable. Fenneman continued: "Many thousands of square miles . . . retain this flatness. In the Llano Estacado or Staked Plains of Texas and New Mexico an area of 20,000 square miles is almost untouched by erosion. North of that [landmark], the drainage from the mountains is directly eastward across the best of the High Plains and the original flat is preserved only between streams."[6]

The Llano Estacado is so level that the elevation differentiation hardly exceeds ten feet per mile. What limited rain nature benevolently bestows occurs "in the late spring and summer, with winter [being] the driest season." In a cyclical pattern of several years, below-average rainfall results in severe drought. Destructive hailstorms frequently disrupt the monotony of the region. Such "capriciousness of moisture and warm temperatures" transformed the Llano Estacado and the adjoining terrain into a land of grass and scrub brush. The conspicuous absence of vertical obstructions such as hills and trees permits the north wind to sweep across the Staked Plains and adjacent land with tremendous velocity. In winter, subzero air from the Rocky Mountains can force temperatures to drop rapidly within hours. These "blue northers" escort "high winds and may carry

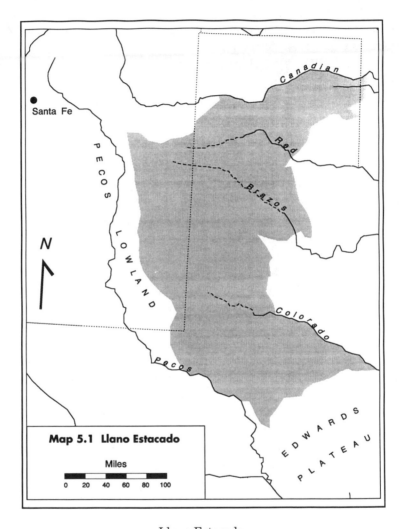

Llano Estacado.

View of El Llano Estacado at the Spade Ranch west of Lubbock,
Texas. Photo courtesy of the Southwest Collection,
Texas Tech University.

moisture or may be dehydrated," causing them to absorb all available
water in their path. Another type of storm characteristic of the Llano
in winter is the catastrophic blizzard, marked by extremely cold temperatures and strong winds that spread snow and ice across the flat
landscape.[7]

Spaniards Encounter the Llano Estacado

In the first half of the sixteenth century, within two generations
after Columbus's voyage of encounter with the Americas, the Spaniards came into this vast, treeless grassland. An initial contributor to
the legacy of sporadic Hispanic presence in the region was Alvar
Núñez Cabeza de Vaca. Shipwrecked on the Texas coast and enslaved
by nomadic Indian tribes, Cabeza de Vaca and three companions
escaped from captivity in 1534 and meandered through the wilderness

of Texas. These Spanish sojourners trudged to the northwest, guided by the sun and the stars, through the High Plains and the Llano Estacado.[8]

Besides the seemingly endless level terrain, their encounter with the *cíbolo*, an animal with "small horns like the cows of Morocco," definitely impressed the wanderers. Cabeza de Vaca later described these animals in his published *Relación*. Their hair, he wrote, was "very long and flocky," like Merinos' wool, and their meat tasted "finer and better than the beef" of Iberia. Avowing that the numerous herds of cíbola had migrated "from as far away as the seacoast of Florida," Don Alvar noted that they grazed "over a tract of more than 400 leagues."[9]

Oral retellings of the adventures of "four ragged castaways" in the interior of the continent — reinforced later by the *Relación* — compelled Viceroy Antonio de Mendoza in Mexico City to consider seriously investigating this wonderland. In search of the Seven Cities of Cíbola, Francisco Vázquez de Coronado led a magnificent cavalcade of explorers through the arid lands of the Southwest and ultimately to the eastern edge of the Llano Estacado.[10] Frustrated in his initial quest for great riches but motivated to discover Quivira, reportedly located east of the Río Pecos, the captain-general sent the main contingent of his army back to the Río Grande in the spring of 1541, while he and a small unit of cavalry, riding the best horses and guided by natives and a compass, entered an "essentially treeless but belegended land."[11]

Accustomed to modest prairies in Spain, these explorers felt uncomfortably confined by the wilderness and were shocked by the flatness of the Staked Plains. Pedro de Castañeda, renowned chronicler of the expedition, described how the vastness of the environment simply overwhelmed them:

> Now we will speak of the plains. The country is spacious and level, and is more than 400 leagues [1,040 miles] wide in the part between the two mountain ranges. . . . No settlements were seen anywhere on these plains. In traversing 250 leagues [650 miles], the other [eastern] mountain range was not seen, nor a hill nor a hillock which was three times as high as a man. Several lakes were found at intervals; they were round as plates; a stone's throw or more across. . . . The grass grows tall near these lakes; away from them it is very short, a span or less. The country is like a bowl, so that when a man sits down, the horizon surrounds him all around at the distance of a musket shot.[12]

As the riders approached the *barrancas* of the Llano Estacado, erratic depressions in the terrain created by countless years of gradual erosion, Castañeda complained about the region's sparse natural resources: "There are no groves of trees except at the rivers, which flow at the bottom of some ravines where the trees grow so thick they were not noticed until one was right on the edge of them. They are of dead earth. There are paths down into these [barrancas], made by the cows [bison] when they go to the water, which is essential throughout these plains."[13] With greater frequency, Coronado's men encountered immense herds of bison the chronicler off-handedly called "cows."

> Another thing worth noticing is that the bulls traveled without cows in such numbers that nobody could have counted them. . . . The country they travelled over was so level and smooth that if one looked at them the sky could be seen between their legs, so that if some of them were at a distance they looked like smooth-trunked pines whose tops joined, and if there was only one bull it looked as if there were four pines. When one was near them, it was impossible to see the ground on the other side of them.[14]

The flatness of the terrain exasperated Castañeda: "It is impossible to find tracks in this country, because the grass straightened up again as soon as it was trodden down."[15] Exasperation often turned to panic whenever members of the expedition became separated from the main party. Castañeda reported that

> many of [the] men who went hunting got lost and were unable to return to the camp for two or three days. They wandered from place to place without knowing how to find their way back. . . . It must be remarked that since the land is so level, when they had wandered aimlessly until noon, following the game, they had to remain by their kill, without straying, until the sun began to go down in order to learn which direction they then had to take to get back to their starting point.[16]

Derivation of "Llano Estacado"

The name "Llano Estacado," which Coronado's explorers applied to the physiography, has eluded precise interpretation. Herbert Eugene Bolton, founder of the Spanish borderlands school of historiography, suggested that as sixteenth-century explorers descended from the highlands of present-day eastern New Mexico they viewed in the distance an "imposing line of rampart-like cliffs" that projected upon the "vast land expanse ahead of them" the visual effect of a stockaded or palisaded plain — *llano estacado* in Spanish. Anglo-Americans later incorrectly translated "llano estacado" into "staked plains," which completely missed the subtle point of the Spaniards' designation.[17] Another explanation, provided by Noel M. Loomis, alluded to a practical solution for a worrisome problem of safeguarding the army's horses: In a varied geographic environment, Spanish pioneers normally secured their remounts "with the aid of the topography," but in the flatness of the Plains they used stakes to tether their horses.[18]

Still a third authority, H. Bailey Carroll, persuasively reasoned that differences had evolved over the meaning or application of the word "estacado," which he interpreted as "staked, enclosed with stakes, palisaded, or possibly stockaded." The upshot of Carroll's perspective is that the Spaniards who named these Staked Plains came from New Mexico rather than Texas. Not without merit was his explanation that the original nomenclature might have been "Llano *Destacado*," "destacado" being the past participle of the verb *destacar*, "to detach from the main body of which it is a part." As applied to the Llano Estacado or Staked Plains, a more pragmatic definition of this verb seemed appropriate: "to emboss, to elevate, to stand out, or to raise." Carroll conceded that such an application of "destacado" was not, strictly speaking, an acceptable literary form; however, to Hispanic wanderers confronted by the reality of the geography, it would have been functional frontier Castilian. In popular usage, New Mexican sojourners, inclined to slur the initial consonant "d," altered the term to "estacado."[19]

Finally, a fourth explanation, attributable to Castañeda of the Coronado expedition, stemmed from an ingenious method used by the Tejas Indians to guide the army across the Llano Estacado on its return trip from the nonexistent Quivira: "Their method of guiding was as follows: early in the morning they watched where the sun rose, then, going in the direction they wanted to take they shot an arrow, and before coming to it they shot another over it, and in this manner they traveled the day."[20] In this explanation, the arrows constituted the "stakes."

Late Colonial Exploration of the Llano Estacado

The termination of Vázquez de Coronado's *entrada* into the northern wilderness effectively closed the age of aggressive conquest. This was followed by a half century of slow, methodical exploration, settlement, and expansion into the central corridor of colonial Mexico, bordered by the eastern and western ranges of the Sierra Madre.[21] Before the close of the sixteenth century, other Hispanic entradas (Rodríguez-Sánchez Chamuscado in 1580, Antonio de Espejo in 1581, and Gaspar Castaño de Sosa in 1590) approached the western slope of the Llano Estacado by way of the Tierra Blanca Creek route.[22] Each expedition blazed new trails, finding in the process three corridors with sources of water: along the Canadian River; from El Paso del Norte over to the Río Pecos and east to the Edwards Plateau country; and through the Bosque Redondo by way of present-day Portales, New Mexico, to the Staked Plains.[23]

Regardless of the avenue of approach, when these intrepid explorers reached the plains of West Texas, the levelness of the Llano Estacado made a profound impression upon them. "These were not ordinary men," concluded Frederick W. Rathjen, "but were men of experience — urbane explorers." As evidenced by written records, the semiarid nature of the Plains did not startle their urbanity; rather, it was the vastness of the terrain, the incredible flatness of the topography, the innumerable herds of bison, and the Indians that elevated the Spaniards' awareness.[24]

At the beginning of the seventeenth century, Spanish frontiersmen out of New Mexico, knowledgeable about the location of scarce watering places, crossed western Texas in pursuit of elusive goals. These, however, did not include permanent settlement. Don Juan de Oñate, colonizer of New Mexico, emulated Vázquez de Coronado in all respects except fanfare and pageantry, entering the High Plains region in 1601 in search of the mythical Quivira. Oñate's entourage comprised more than seventy men, a remuda in excess of seven hundred horses and mules, six *carretas* plus two additional carts loaded with four artillery pieces (all drawn by mules), and sufficient teamsters to oversee the transport of "necessary baggage." In an official report to the government, Oñate recalled: "At the entrance of the plains called Cíbola, . . . we found it hard to move the carts, but crossed this difficult pass without trouble through the skill of the good soldiers in charge and reached some very extensive and delightful plains, where we could not even see any mountain range like those we have passed."[25] Awed by the countless bison, Oñate, like the explorers of half a century before, expressed amazement with the environment:

> Proceeding on our way . . . we saw the first of the monstrous Cíbola cattle, [of] which, although they are extremely fleet, we . . . killed four or five bulls, which caused great rejoicing. On the following day, marching ahead, we saw large herds of bulls and cows. From there on we found so many of them that it will be difficult for anyone who has not seen them to believe it, for according to the guess of everyone in the army, wherever we went we saw as many cattle every day as one finds on the largest cattle ranches in New Spain. They were so tame that unless chased or frightened they stood still and did not run away.[26]

Scion of a Zacatecas family in which silver mining and cattle raising were complementary enterprises, Oñate described the cíbola in great detail:

> The meat of these cattle is far superior to our own beef. These animals are very fat, particularly the cows. We learned by experience that one does not tire of their meat as of ours, nor is it in the least harmful.
>
> These cattle are all brown in color. . . . their shape is so amazing that we cannot help but believe that it is the result of the crossing of different animals.[27]

With the conclusion of the Oñate expedition, a lengthy period of Spanish exploration in the northern borderlands ended. The experiences of these adventurers, recorded in a corpus of documentary sources, constituted a frame of reference that succeeding frontier generations could consult.

Christianization and Economic Reconnaissance

Throughout the seventeenth century, other expeditions, less magnificent than Oñate's but all the same led by redoubtable frontier settlers and explorers, continued traversing the High Plains and the Llano Estacado. In 1629, for example, in response to solicitations from Jumano Indians of the lower Texas plains, Franciscan missionaries from Isleta in central New Mexico explored the region east of the Pecos. They hoped to convince the native population to exchange its nomadic existence for the security of structured pueblo life. Friars Juan de Salas and Diego López, accompanied by three soldiers, followed Jumano emissaries to their tribal homeland along the Río Concho to recruit neophytes for Mission San Isidro in New Mexico. Within three years, however, the Jumano neophytes abandoned the mission and migrated back to the Texas plains. In 1632, hoping to persuade at least a few Jumanos to return to Mission San Isidro, Friar Salas briefly visited the Río Concho basin before retreating to New Mexico. Another friar, Juan de Ortega, showed a bit more determination, staying six months among the Jumanos before returning to the Río Grande. For the next eighteen years, converting the Jumanos of Texas remained a low priority with leaders of church and state.[28]

In 1634, Captain Alonso de Vaca led a troop of soldiers out of Santa Fe and traveled eastward for approximately three hundred leagues in search of Quivira. Using the Canadian River as a route of penetration, de Vaca meandered across much of the Llano Estacado, subsisting mainly on cíbolo meat. After marching aimlessly for some three hundred leagues, Alonso de Vaca's disappointed and exhausted party headed back to New Mexico.[29]

For more than a decade after 1634 New Mexican leaders, preoccupied with more demanding problems of defense and survival, generally ignored the mystery of the Llano Estacado. During a lull in frontier administration in 1650, Governor Hernando de la Concha assigned two army captains, Hernán Martín and Diego del Castillo, to lead an expedition to the Río Concho Basin at the southern extension of the Great Plains. Accompanied by soldiers and Christian Indians, the captains blazed a different route from that of previous expeditions until they arrived at the Concho, homeland of the Jumanos. Here the New Mexicans found pecan trees along the river banks and shells in the water containing pearls of modest quality. Inspired by dual motives of curiosity and economics, the Martín-Castillo group followed the Río Concho for a distance and then plodded eastward to the humid timberlands inhabited by the Tejas Indians, who practiced a combination of planting and hunting. Their curiosity satisfied, the explorers retraced their route to the Concho and then traversed the lower Plains back to Santa Fe.[30]

The report of the Martín-Castillo entrada, personally carried to Mexico City by the robust captains and Franciscan leader Fray Antonio de Aranda, greatly stimulated viceregal officials' interest in the Llano. In short order, Viceroy Luis Enríquez de Guzmán, Conde de

Alba de Liste, instructed Governor de la Concha to dispatch a new entrada to assess "the country, its people, and its resources." Accordingly, in 1654 a sizable contingent of thirty soldiers and two hundred Christian Pueblo auxiliaries followed Sgt. Maj. Diego de Guadalajara over the route blazed by the Martín-Castillo expedition to the Río Concho. After establishing temporary field headquarters among the Jumanos, Guadalajara sent a smaller patrol to explore the surrounding territory. Commanded by Capt. Andrés López, the subordinate unit consisted of twelve Spanish soldiers and a number of Pueblo warriors and Jumano allies. Moving east from the Concho, the party encountered resistance at a *ranchería* inhabited by aggressive Cuitaos, who blocked the Spaniards' advance. In the ensuing battle, the Spaniards' superiority of weapons and manpower overwhelmed the Cuitaos, who promptly surrendered. López's party seized "many bundles of deer and buffalo skins" and rejoined Guadalajara at the Río Concho.[31]

The principal objective of his expedition having been fulfilled, the sergeant major, fearful of an Indian response, ordered his soldiers and Pueblo auxiliaries to prepare for the return trip to Santa Fe, leaving the Jumanos at their tribal grounds on the Río Concho. Notwithstanding their brevity, the López and Martín-Castillo expeditions provided the Spaniards of New Mexico with a better understanding of the Llano Estacado and its inhabitants.[32]

Although documentary records are unavailable, Hispanic New Mexicans may have maintained sporadic contact with the Jumano Indians throughout the 1660s and 1670s. It is quite plausible that the Hispanos frequented the Río Concho Basin for trade and friendship in relative safety. According to Frederick W. Rathjen, these expeditions, though small and unimpressive in comparison to the wilderness pageants of earlier years, served as important barometers of the Spaniards' exploration skills and knowledge of the region. The thoroughness of their geographic understanding "is indicated by the fact that in order to cross the Llano Estacado, knowledge of fresh water holes was imperative — and the Spaniards crossed the Staked Plains at will."[33]

Military Expeditions

The Pueblo Revolt of 1680 temporarily ruptured Spanish contact with the plains of West Texas. In 1683 a baptized Jumano, Don Juan Sabaeta, arrived at El Paso del Norte, capital of the Spanish colony-in-exile, requesting assistance for his people. Sabaeta asked Governor Domingo Jironza Petriz de Cruzate for missionaries as well as trade and military protection against hostile Apache foes. The next year a joint military-missionary entrada directed by Capt. Juan Domínguez de Mendoza and Fray Nicolás López reopened contact with the Jumanos of the Río Concho. A sudden French encroachment on the Texas coast during the midpoint of the decade, however, shifted Spanish officials' attention from the Jumanos to the tribes of central and east Texas.[34] It was not until Don Diego de Vargas reconquered New Mexico in 1692, suppressing the final embers of Pueblo insurrection in 1696, that Spanish authorities once more could focus on the High Plains region.[35]

Diego de Vargas's reconquest of New Mexico, followed quickly by the onset of Bourbon rule in Spain, constituted a dramatic shift in colonial policy on the Staked Plains. Although it was several years before Hispanic frontier leaders discerned the change, by 1700 there had emerged "an odd dichotomy" of beneficial trade counterbalanced by aggressive defensive warfare.[36] Military activity was aimed at thwarting French intrusion and Indian expansion fomented by the Comanches, who claimed the southern Plains as their new national territory.[37] Pushed out of the Panhandle, the Lipan Apaches, who depended on the cíbolo for subsistence, migrated east and south until their hunting forays brought them into conflict with Spanish settlements in Texas and Coahuila.[38]

Aside from punitive campaigns against Indian marauders (such as that directed by New Mexico Governor Pedro Rodríguez Cubero against Apache strongholds in the Panhandle), Spaniards stayed away from the Staked Plains country in the early eighteenth century. Though the New Mexicans had only limited successes in their campaigns, the sporadic conflict continued. Compounding the situation for Hispanic leaders in both New Mexico and Texas was the serious threat of Comanche warfare. In fact, the severity of Comanche raiding intensified throughout the middle decades of the eighteenth century.[39] The fighting was accented occasionally by periods of erratic peace, during which native raiders traded stolen goods and human captives at concealed contact points along watercourses, in the eastern canyons of the Llano Estacado, and at other locations in West Texas.[40]

Communication Lines Across the Llano Estacado

The Treaty of Paris of 1763 eliminated France as a colonial power in North America, awarding Spain the territory west of the Mississippi River plus the city of New Orleans. However, the Hispanos' problems with Indian confrontations in the Borderlands remained unresolved. The villas of Santa Fe and San Antonio de Béjar constituted terminal points in a defense structure that stretched in an arc from New Mexico to Texas. Prominently located within this territory were the High Plains and the Llano Estacado. Hispanic leaders generally acknowledged the necessity of establishing communication linkages between the two provinces; they also perceived the Comanches as a barrier to the opening of another branch of *el camino real*, connecting Santa Fe with San Antonio.

To demonstrate that the Comanche barrier could be penetrated, Pedro Vial, a Hispanicized Frenchman, conducted three expeditions beginning in 1786 "designed to establish direct routes" between the two provinces. The year after Vial's first expedition, José Mares, a retired corporal from New Mexico, left Santa Fe and traversed the Llano Estacado in an effort to shorten the distance of the trail Vial had blazed earlier. Other Hispanos also approached the Staked Plains country in the twilight years of the eighteenth century and the initial decade of the nineteenth century — not to search for settlement sites but to explore potential routes of travel between New Mexico and Texas. For instance, cavalrymen Santiago Fernández and Francisco Xavier Fragoso, accompanied by three New Mexicans, escorted Pedro Vial through the Llano Estacado on a return trip from Santa Fe to San Antonio in 1788–89. In 1808, to reinforce frontier defenses of Spanish Texas, sexagenarian Capt. Francisco Amangual, commanding a force of two hundred men on a tour of peace, traveled around the eastern slope of the Llano Estacado to the Canadian River and ultimately arrived in Santa Fe.

These expeditions illustrated that Hispanos possessed a great deal of applied knowledge of Borderlands geography, particularly about the West Texas plains and the Llano Estacado. José Mares apparently was the first Hispanic New Mexican to penetrate the Llano since the Martín-Castillo entrada of 1650. Despite over 130 years of inactivity, the Llano Estacado continued to intrigue but not to discourage a new generation of frontier Spaniards.[41]

Correcting the Myth of Hispanic Failure

Although Hispanos traversed the vast expanse of the West Texas plains at various times throughout the colonial period, they never established permanent settlements. They did not fail to do so because they lacked initiative, imagination, or courage. Rather, they avoided the uninviting region because of the absence of dependable sources of water and because of the exposed, unprotected nature of the terrain. In contrast to Frederick W. Rathjen, who acknowledged both the virtues and failings of Spanish frontier folk in the West Texas plains, Walter Prescott Webb and other scholars have not been so sensitive. In his celebrated treatise *The Great Plains*, Webb unabashedly proclaimed:

> In surveying the Spanish activities in the Great Plains region from 1528 to 1848, the end of the Spanish-Mexican régime, it becomes clear that the Spaniards enjoyed unusual success as explorers, but that they were notably unsuccessful as colonists. Their lack of success has often been attributed to conditions in Europe or to some defect in the Spanish colonial system. A reexamination of the evidence seems to indicate that the Spanish failure to take and hold the Great Plains may be attributed . . . to the nature of the problems found within the country, and not to the European situation.[42]

Regarding the Spaniards' response to Indians, Webb concluded: "At the end of the Spanish régime the Plains Indians were more powerful, far richer, and in control of more territory than they were at the beginning of it. The problem of subduing them had to be solved by another race."[43]

Another writer, J. Evetts Haley, conceded to the Spanish frontiersmen one lone virtue, a lusty vigor that derived from their dependence on red meat:

> Before the coming of the cowboy, before the buffalo hunters straggled in, and even before the earliest Anglo-American explorers came, the Panhandle of Texas was known to the Span-

iard and the Mexican. To the plains, the Spanish buffalo hunters or *ciboleros* came annually from the little New Mexican villages shut off from the rest of the world, and hunted, not with high-powered rifles, but with betasseled lances and fleet ponies. Thus they put up their winter's meat, and at times brought hard-baked loaves of bread and other articles to trade with the Indians. But the more extensive trading was the work of the Indian traders — the *Comancheros*.[44]

Statements such as these definitely compounded the myth that Hispanics lacked the determination and fortitude to succeed as settlers and incorporate the Staked Plains under Spanish rule. Admittedly, during the Spanish colonial period few settlers either out of Texas or New Mexico occupied land in the region owing to the desolate isolation, lack of reliable water, diplomacy from Madrid, and, in the later decades of the eighteenth century, Comanche hostility. Notwithstanding the paucity of settlers, however, the truth is that the Spanish possessed the resolve to crisscross the Llano Estacado and the Staked Plains, and they left ample evidence of their transitory presence in other ways. "The most obvious remnants of Spanish occupation in the Southwest," avowed Andrés Tijerina, "are the artifacts, words, and customs."[45] Geography retains a clear measure of the Hispanic past in such names as Agua Corriente (running water), Alamocitos (little cottonwoods), Cañón Casas Amarillas (yellow cliffs like city walls canyon), Cañón de la Punta de Agua (source of water canyon), Cañón de Rescate (ransom negotiations — between Indian traders and Hispanos — canyon), Cañón Frío (cold water draw), Cañón Tierra Blanca (white earth draw), Laguna Plata (silvery reflection in water), Los Escarbados (diggings or scrapings), Los Tules (reeds) Canyon, Palo Duro (hard or dry wood) Canyon, Sierrita de la Cruz (little hill of the cross), Tascosa (actually *atascosa*, a boggy or muddy place), and several others.[46]

Indicative of the colonial activity that contributed to place-name geography was an old Spanish armor found near the western slope of the Llano Estacado in 1870. U.S. Army Capt. John G. Bourke, recipient of the artifact, speculated on its origin: "This armor was simple in style and construction and no doubt once covered the body of a Spanish or Mexican foot-soldier, who must have lost his life while on some expedition of discovery or war, years and years ago." Bourke concluded: "The age of his armor I never could learn; it was of the style used by the infantry in the 17th and 18th century, but may have been of any period prior to our occupation of Texas and New Mexico. Its preservation from rust is attributable to the extremely dry climate of the staked plains, where rain falls so seldom."[47]

The Beginning of Permanent Hispanic Settlement

Shortly after the end of the Civil War, the U.S. government assigned cavalry units to end Indian conflict in the trans-Mississippi West. As the threat of Indian hostility subsided, Hispanics from New Mexico began to migrate into the High Plains and the Llano Estacado of West Texas, first in search of grazing land and then as permanent settlers. Coinciding with the arrival of Captain Bourke and his soldiers in New Mexico, signaling the advent of peace, the Cabeza de Baca brothers (Aniceto, José, Pablo, and Simón) descended the highlands from Upper Las Vegas, crossed the Río Pecos, and ascended the Llano Estacado with their flocks of sheep."[48] Hence began serious occupation of the West Texas plains by Hispanic homesteaders. By the turn of the century, hardy people such as José Ynocencio Romero represented the next generation of sheepmen to remain on the Staked Plains.[49]

Although dependable sources of water were not located until 1937, when drillers successfully tapped underground reservoirs,[50] those Hispanics who finally settled in the region in the 1870s, long after the end of the colonial period, appreciated the economic advantage of uniting sheep with the sea of grass of the West Texas plains.

Notes

The author wishes to express his deep gratitude to Professors Frederick W. Rathjen and Garry L. Nall of West Texas State A & M University at Canyon for their helpful assistance with perspectives and materials for this essay.

1. J. W. Williams, "Coronado: From the Río Grande to the Concho," *Southwestern Historical Quarterly* 63 (October 1959): 206.

2. Libro IV, Título VII, De la población de las ciudades, villas y pueblos, *Recopilación de leyes de los reynos de las Indias*, 4 vols. (Madrid: Julián de Paredes, 1681; rpt. Madrid: Ediciones Cultura Hispánica, 1973), 2: 90.

3. Warren A. Beck, *New Mexico: History of Four Centuries* (Norman: University of Oklahoma Press, 1962), pp. 52-60; Félix D. Almaráz, Jr., *The San Antonio Missions and Their System of Land Tenure* (Austin: University of Texas Press, 1989), pp. 1-7.

4. Elmer H. Johnson, *The Natural Regions of Texas*, University of Texas Bureau of Research Monograph No. 8 (Austin: University of Texas, 1931), p. 51.

5. W. C. Holden, "The Land," in Lawrence L. Graves, ed., *A History of Lubbock* (Lubbock: West Texas Museum Association/Texas Technological College, 1962), pp. 5-6.

6. Nevin H. Fenneman, *Physiography of Western United States* (New York: McGraw-Hill Book Company, Inc., 1931), p. 14.

7. Georgellen Burnett, *We Just Toughed It Out: Women in the Llano Estacado*, Southwestern Studies No. 90 (El Paso: Texas Western Press, 1990), p. 2.

8. Beck, *New Mexico*, p. 42.

9. Cyclone Covey, trans. and ed., *Cabeza de Vaca's Adventures in the Unknown Interior of America*, repr. ed. (Albuquerque: University of New Mexico Press, 1983), p. 81, quoted in Sandra L. Myers, "What Kind of Animal Be This?" *Western Historical Quarterly* 20 (February, 1989): 5.

10. Herbert E. Bolton, *Coronado: Knight of Pueblos and Plains* (Albuquerque: University of New Mexico Press, 1949), pp. 8-22, 49-80.

11. J. Evetts Haley, *The XIT Ranch of Texas and the Early Days of the Llano Estacado* (Norman: University of Oklahoma Press, 1967), p. 7; William B. Conroy, "The Llano Estacado in 1541: Spanish Perception of a Distinctive Physical Setting," *Journal of the West* 11 (October 1972): 576.

12. "The Coronado Expedition, 1540-1541: Castañeda's Description of the High Plains", in Ernest Wallace and David M. Vigness, eds., *Documents of Texas History*, (Austin: The Steck Company, 1963), pp. 5-6.

13. Ibid.

14. Ibid.

15. Pedro de Castañeda, "The Narrative of the Expedition of Coronado," in Frederick W. Hodge, ed., *Spanish Explorers in the Southern United States, 1528–1543*, repr. ed. (New York: Charles Scribner's Sons, 1907; rpt. Austin: Texas State Historical Association, 1984), pp. 330-31.

16. George P. Hammond and Agapito Rey, eds. and trans., *Narratives of the Coronado Expedition, 1540–1542* (Albuquerque: University of New Mexico Press, 1940), p. 241.

17. Bolton, *Coronado*, p. 243.

18. Noel M. Loomis and Abraham P. Nasatir, *Pedro Vial and the Roads to Santa Fe* (Norman: University of Oklahoma Press, 1967), p. 493n.

19. H. Bailey Carroll, "Llano Estacado," in *The Handbook of Texas*, 3 vols. (Austin: Texas State Historical Association, 1952-1976), 2: 70.

20. Hammond and Rey, *Narratives of the Coronado Expedition*, p. 242.

21. Félix D. Almaráz, Jr., "Spain's Cultural Legacy in Texas," in Ben Procter and Archie P. McDonald, eds., *The Texas Heritage* (Arlighton Heights, IL: Harlan Davidson, Inc., 1992), p. 6.

22. Herbert Eugene Bolton and Thomas Maitland Marshall, *The Colonization of North America, 1492–1783* (New York: The Macmillan Company, 1920), p. 72; George P. Hammond and Agapito Rey, eds. and trans., *The Rediscovery of New Mexico, 1580–1594* (Albuquerque: University of New Mexico Press, 1966), pp. 6-40.

23. Williams, "Coronado: From the Río Grande to the Concho," p. 20.

24. Frederick W. Rathjen, *The Texas Panhandle Frontier* (Austin: University of Texas Press, 1973), pp. 59-60.

25. George P. Hammond and Agapito Rey, eds. and trans., *Don Juan de Oñate: Colonizer of New Mexico*, 2 vols. (Albuquerque: University of New Mexico Press, 1953), 1: 24-25.

26. "Juan de Oñate, Faithful and True Report . . . in this Year of 1601," in ibid., 2: 749-750.

27. Ibid., 2: 750.

28. Rathjen, *Texas Panhandle Frontier*, pp. 66-67; W. C. Holden, "Indians, Spaniards, and Anglos," in *A History of Lubbock*, pp. 25-28.

29. Carlos E. Castañeda, *Our Catholic Heritage in Texas, 1519–1936*, 7 vols. (Austin: Von Boeckmann-Jones Company, 1936), 1: 204.

30. Ibid., 1: 204-205.

31. Ibid., 1: 206.

32. Rathjen, *Texas Panhandle Frontier*, pp. 67-68.

33. Ibid., p. 68.

34. Ibid., pp. 68-69; Almaráz, "Spain's Cultural Legacy, pp. 6-8.

35. J. Manuel Espinosa, *Crusaders of the Río Grande: The Story of Don Diego de Vargas and the Reconquest and Refounding of New Mexico* (Chicago: Institute of Jesuit History, 1942), pp. 49-87; J. Manuel Espinosa, trans. and ed., *The Pueblo Indian Revolt of 1696 and the Franciscan Missions in New Mexico: Letters of the Missionaries and Related Documents* (Norman: University of Oklahoma Press, 1988), pp. 32-58.

36. Rathjen, *Texas Panhandle Frontier*, p. 69.

37. Ibid., p. 71.

38. Thomas F. Schilz, *Lipan Apaches in Texas*, Southwestern Studies No. 83 (El Paso: Texas Western Press, 1987), p. 7.

39. Rathjen, *Texas Panhandle Frontier*, p. 72.

40. L. R. Bailey, *Indian Slave Trade in the Southwest* (Los Angeles: Westernlore Press, 1973), pp. 24-26; Charles L. Kenner, *A History of New Mexican–Plains Indian Relations* (Norman: University of Oklahoma Press, 1969), pp. 23-52.

41. Rathjen, *Texas Panhandle Frontier*, pp. 77-81.

42. Walter Prescott Webb, *The Great Plains* (Waltham, MA: Blaisdell Publishing Company, 1931), p. 85.

43. Ibid., p. 183.

44. Haley, *The XIT Ranch of Texas*, p. 18.

45. Andrés A. Tijerina, *History of Mexican Americans in Lubbock County, Texas*, Graduate Studies No. 18 (Lubbock: Texas Tech University Press, 1979), p. 8.

46. Holden, "Indians, Spaniards, and Anglos," *History of Lubbock*, pp. 27-30.

47. Lansing B. Bloom, ed., "Bourke on the Southwest, II — Winning His Spurs," *New Mexico Historical Review* 9 (January 1934): 46.

48. Fabiola Cabeza de Baca, *We Fed Them Cactus* (Albuquerque: University of New Mexico Press, 1954), p. x.

49. Ernest R. Archambeau, "Spanish Sheepmen on the Canadian at Old Tascosa, by José Ynocencio Romero," *Panhandle-Plains Historical Review* 19 (1946): 45-73.

50. Henry Charles Miller, "The Role of Water in the Settlement of the Llano Estacado" (M.A. thesis, University of Texas at Austin, 1960), p. 179.

†

6
The Villasur Expedition and the Segesser Hide Paintings

Thomas E. Chávez

The Segesser hide paintings are among the most novel and important artifacts of Spain's colonial history in New Mexico and the Great Plains. As aesthetic works they are striking; as hide paintings they are unique; and as historical documents they have sparked revisions in interpretation of the period, providing valuable information on modes of warfare, uniforms and clothing, and the war panoply of the Plains Indians. Now housed in the Museum of New Mexico at the Palace of the Governors, the Segesser paintings bring together more than two and a half centuries of history.

History

In 1758, Father Philipp von Segesser von Brunegg, a Jesuit priest stationed in the province of Sonora, sent three "colored skins," or hide paintings, to his brother in Switzerland.[1] Until recently, two of them remained in the possession of the Segesser family. Now these paintings, which depict Spaniards and Frenchmen as well as Oto, Pawnee, Apache, and Pueblo Indians, have returned to North America. By his act long ago, Father Segesser set in motion a series of events that would span several centuries, The paintings' return ties the present to events that occurred a half century before the hides were shipped to the Old World.

During the first decades of the eighteenth century, New Spain's northern province of New Mexico was a source of increasing consternation to Spanish officials in Mexico City. New Mexico had just suffered a major Indian rebellion — the Pueblo Revolt of 1680 — that had prevented any Spanish settlement for thirteen years. By 1693 New Mexico's governor, Diego de Vargas, finally succeeded in resuming colonization, but he was impeded in his plan for pacification by constant Indian raids and Spanish political infighting.

New Mexico was an important link in New Spain's northern line of defense. The province had become an advance bulwark against the pressures of Indian nationalism. It was also theoretically a bastion against the western pretensions of the French, who had established themselves in the lower Mississippi Valley and the Illinois country and who were competing with the Spanish for control of the trans-Mississippi West. A battle resulting from this Spanish-French rivalry is the subject of one of the Segesser hide paintings, and both it and its companion depict confrontations involving Indians.

Evidence of a French presence west of the Mississippi River prior to 1719 is sketchy. On a historic voyage, René-Robert Cavalier, sieur de La Salle, tried to establish a French settlement at the mouth of the Mississippi River in 1684. However, he sailed beyond his intended destination, put ashore at Matagorda Bay on the Texas coast, and was eventually murdered by his own men. His settlement of 180 people failed, with only about half a dozen people surviving. One of these was seventeen-year-old Jean L'Archévèque, who allegedly had helped kill La Salle. L'Archévèque was eventually found by the Spaniards: he gave testimony in Mexico and later moved to Santa Fe, where he became a well-known merchant.[2] By the 1690s, French coureurs des bois (explorers, traders, and trappers) had traveled along the lower reaches of the Missouri River and probably farther west onto the Plains. A series of maps published by Frenchman Guillaume Delisle adds further evidence of French intrusion into Spanish territory. In a 1703 map, Delisle correctly placed the Pawnees but did not note the Apaches, whom the French called "Padoucas." Two of his subsequent maps, dated 1718 and 1722, accurately located both Indian groups, however. Yet none of his maps noted El Cuartelejo, a settlement of New Mexican Pueblo and Apache Indians near today's Colorado-Kansas border.[3]

As early as 1702, a memoir of Pierre LeMoyne, sieur d'Iberville, mentioned a number of Missouri River tribes, the most important of

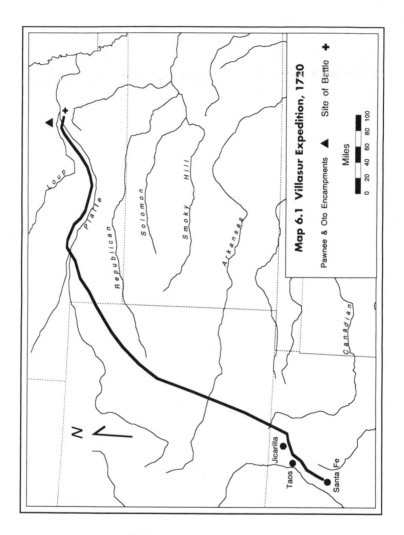

Villasur Expedition, 1720.

Father Philipp von Segesser von Brunegg, S.J. (1689–1762).
Painting in private collection of Segesser family,
Lucerne, Switzerland.

which were the Oto Indians, neighbors of the Pawnees. Other reports indicated that the French undoubtedly knew of New Mexico and its mines. One French map, based on a report by a former New Mexican governor, Diego de Peñalosa, contains a cartouche of Indians working in mines.[4] Word of French influence expanding onto the north central Plains traveled among the Indians and reached New Mexico, where it was picked up by expeditions northeast of Santa Fe and Taos. New Mexico's governors relayed this information to Mexico City.[5]

In 1706, Juan de Ulibarrí led an expedition to bring back some recalicitrant Pueblo Indians from El Cuartelejo. He returned with more news: The Pueblos had, in effect, aligned themselves to the Cuartelejo Apaches. The Apaches invited Ulibarrí and his soldiers to join them in making war on the Pawnees and their French allies. To drive the point home, the Apaches showed Ulibarrí French trade goods and weapons captured from the Pawnees.[6] Ulibarrí declined the invitation but questioned the Apaches about the geography of the plains beyond Cuartelejo before returning to Santa Fe to make his report.

New Mexico also suffered incessant Apache and Comanche attacks. A series of expeditions was dispatched to restrain these Indians. In 1714 Governor de Vargas's old friend and colleague, Juan Páez Hurtado, led onto the Plains a major expedition of more than 200 men, including 146 Pueblo Indian auxiliaries from at least nine different pueblos. Hurtado's mission was to quell the raiding and counterraiding among Plains Indians, which disrupted alliances the Spanish had forged among the various tribes. Suspicion was growing that the French had instigated much of this agitation.[7]

Páez Hurtado was guided by Joseph Naranjo, who seems to have been used on most, if not all, expeditions of the period. A native of Santa Clara Pueblo, Naranjo was a famous scout and warrior, and the Spanish paid him an unusual tribute by granting him the official title of "chief war captain" of all Pueblo auxiliary troops. The Páez Hurtado expedition went down the Canadian River to somewhere around the present location of Amarillo, Texas. No contact was made with Indians, nor did the party see any evidence of French intrusion.[8] Nonetheless, the New Mexicans had grounds for concern.

Four years later, Frenchman Charles Claude Du Tisné tried to make contact with the Padouca Apaches and the Comanches. The ranges of both, he realized, bordered on New Mexico. Drawing on information from his countryman Étiene Véniard, sieur de Bourgmont, who had traveled up the Missouri River to the Arikara/Pawnee villages and thence up the Platte River into Wyoming, Du Tisné traveled southwest into Osage country and then into southern Pawnee country (today's northern Oklahoma). In the process he traded all his firearms and received, among other things, a mule with a Spanish brand.[9] New Mexicans heard of Du Tisné's visit to the southern Pawnees almost before he returned. The Comanches were disturbed about their Pawnee neighbors' having muskets and conveyed the information to the Spanish.

Eventually, reports of French activity in present-day Texas, coupled with New Mexico's already existing problems, convinced the authorities in Mexico City that action had to be taken. The Spanish viceroy, Baltasar de Zuñiga, Marqués de Valero, instructed New Mexico Governor Antonio Valverde y Cossío to establish a mission among the friendly Jicarilla Apaches on the eastern slope of the Santa Fe (now Sangre de Cristo) Mountains around present-day Cimarron, New Mexico. Valverde was also instructed to establish a presidio at El Cuartelejo. Although the governor understood the frightening implications of French intrusion and acknowledged the viceroy's instructions, he concentrated on organizing a punitive expedition against the Comanches, who had just raided some New Mexican settlements. Valverde intended to seek information about the French while he was on the Plains. In 1719 he left Santa Fe with 60 garrison troops, 40 settlers, and 465 auxiliary Indians. On this expedition, he did find irrefutable evidence of a French presence on the Plains. Once back home, Valverde convened a council to evaluate the new evidence and reconsider the viceroy's instructions.[10]

Viceroy Valero had learned from Madrid that a state of war existed between France and Spain. With the subsequent loss of Pensacola to France in 1719, the viceroy became convinced of a mounting French threat on the Plains. New Mexico needed to act. But despite the urgency of the situation, Valverde and his council could not agree with the viceroy's orders. A presidio at El Cuartelejo was deemed unfeasible because of expense and distance from Santa Fe. A more practical plan would be the establishment of a mission at La Jicarilla, near present-day Cimarron, and another major expedition to reconnoiter the French.[11]

In mid-June 1720, Valverde dispatched an expedition under the leadership of his lieutenant governor, Pedro de Villasur. Approximately forty-two royal troops, three civilians, and sixty Pueblo Indians headed northeast to ascertain the location and strength of the French

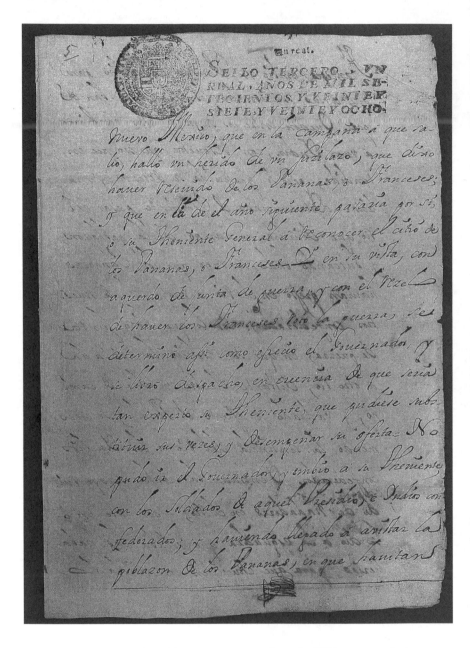

Testimony dated 29 May 1729 stating that the Villasur expedition
left Santa Fe to reconnoiter the Pawnee Indians and their French
allies. No 490, Spanish Archives of New Mexico, State Records
Center and Archives, Santa Fe.

(see Fig. 6.2). Expatriate Frenchman Jean L'Archévèque (now Juan de Archibeque) went along as an interpreter, for the Spanish really believed they would encounter Frenchmen.

The Spanish went to Taos, through Jicarilla and south of present-day Raton, and on to El Cuartelejo, where they picked up some Padouca allies. They continued in a northeasterly direction toward the Platte River (Río de Jesús María) in present eastern Nebraska and followed it east to the Loup River (Río San Lorenzo), where they found evidence of a large Indian village on the move. The party continued up the Loup until it came to a Pawnee encampment. Villasur tried to open dialogue with the Indians, but to no avail. When he heard from a number of sources that a white man was living among the Pawnees, he attempted to contact the man with a letter written in French by L'Archévèque. Again, no answer.

Sensing a potentially dangerous situation, Villasur ordered his army to retreat to the confluence of the Loup and Platte rivers, where the men set up camp on a grassy plain. At daybreak of the next day, 14 August 1720, the Pawnees and their Oto allies slipped across the river and attacked. Their surprise assault caught the New Mexicans badly disorganized. The Indians' initial volley apparently included some musket shots, deadly proof that they had indeed obtained firearms from the French. A major battle ensued, in which all but thirteen of the Spanish were left dead in the tall grass. Villasur, L'Archévèque, and the expedition's only priest, Father Juan Mínguez, all perished.[12] Naranjo, the famous scout, was among the Pueblo allies killed.

The ambush was a major catastrophe for New Mexico, claiming a third of the province's best soldiers. A former governor, Félix Martínez, who was Valverde's rival and antagonist, wrote to Viceroy Valero: "In the villa of Santa Fe, thirty-two widows and many orphaned children, whose tears reach the sky, mourn the poor ability of the governor, pray God for his punishment, and await the remedy of your justice."[13] Martínez was already in Mexico City facing various charges resulting from his term as governor. The result of his letter was a series of reports and interviews. Valverde defended Villasur, whom Martínez accused of incompetence and inexperience. The investigation continued for the next seven years.

Valverde reported that Frenchmen participated in the battle, although Felipe Tamaris, one of the survivors, testified that he did not know who was involved. The investigation culminated in a mild reprimand for Valverde: He was ordered to pay 50 pesos toward charity

Detail of the attacking cavalry in Segesser I. With the exception
of some of the headdresses, all the clothing, armor, and weapons
are Spanish, but the pronghorns indicate that the site may
have been the Great Plains. Segesser File, courtesy of the
Museum of New Mexico, Palace of the Governors.

masses for the souls of the dead soldiers and 150 pesos for the purchase of a chalice and ornaments for new missions. The same order
absolved Valverde of guilt for his judgment in choosing Villasur to lead
the expedition.[14]

Discovery

Almost forty years after the catastrophic Villasur expedition,
Father Segesser sent his gift of three colored skins to Switzerland. His
correspondence gave no indication that he knew the paintings
depicted battles fought by Villasur and his men or other Spanish/

Detail of Pedro de Villasur in Segesser II. The dead Villasur is
depicted in an officer's coat, lying on his back behind an officer's
tent and bleeding out of his mouth. The officer standing over
him is José Domínguez. Courtesy of the Museum of
New Mexico, Palace of the Governors.

Pueblo expeditions. Nor did his writings indicate how the hide paintings had come into his possession; he merely described them as curiosities.[15]

Over the centuries, all of Father Segesser's letters and two of the
three paintings remained in the possession of the Segesser family.
Those letters and family tradition have helped establish the prove-
nance of the paintings: Ownership can be traced all the way back to
Father Segesser's brother. During the past century several changes in
ownership occurred. In 1894 Heinrich Viktor von , Segesser-Crivelli

Dr. and Mrs. André von Segesser, Lucerne, Switzerland, 1985.
Segesser File, courtesy of the Museum of New Mexico,
Palace of the Governors, Santa Fe.

sold the paintings to Paul von Segesser, the trustee of the Segesser Palace, who in turn left them to his son, Joseph Leopold. Joseph left them to his son Hans Ulrich von Segesser, who left them to his nephew Dr. André von Segesser.

The paintings might have disappeared altogether had it not been for Gottfried Hotz, a scholar and former seminarian at Küsnacht in Zürich Canton. A professor of the Geographical-Ethnological Society of the Geological Society of Zürich, Hotz was also curator at the North American Indian Museum in Zürich. He became the connecting link between the eighteenth-century New Mexican expeditions, the paintings, Father Segesser, and the present.

Hotz first learned of the existence of the paintings in 1945. With the cooperation of Hans Ulrich von Segesser and his mother, Josefina von Segesser, Hotz devoted himself to the complex task of establishing the origin of the paintings. He traveled to the United States and Mexico and explored every potential source of information. His inquiries sparked the interest of the Museum of New Mexico, whose curators apparently did not know of the paintings. Dr. Bertha Dutton, curator of ethnology at the Museum of New Mexico, first received Hotz's inquiries and referred them to E. Boyd, curator of Spanish colonial art at the Museum of International Folk Art, a branch of the Museum of New Mexico. Boyd wrote Hotz in 1960, "It is most fortunate that the two paintings . . . were sent to the Segesser family in Switzerland, where they have been preserved." She soon indicated that she wanted the paintings brought to Santa Fe: "Dr. Wedel [of the Smithsonian Institution] and I would very much like to see the pictures brought to the United States . . . for exhibition."[16]

Boyd and Santa Fe author Oliver LaFarge became very interested in the paintings and kept up a long correspondence with Hotz. LaFarge wrote, "Miss Boyd and I are agreed that, whatever their actual origin, these paintings may be of great historical importance." He added that Hotz had "made a real contribution in calling attention to these paintings." Some scholars were less restrained in expressing their interest: One of Boyd's colleagues gushed that news of the paintings had her in a "tizzy" and that "if you [Boyd] get them in your mitts . . . I'm drooling."[17]

After spending years researching eighteenth-century Spanish expeditions, Indian nations, geography, and colonial art, Hotz published some conclusions in a 1958 book titled, *Indianische Fellmalereien Aus Schweizer Privatbesitz*. In 1970, the University of

Oklahoma Press issued an English translation of the work, *Indian Skin Paintings from the American Southwest: Two Representatives of Border Conflicts Between Mexico and the Missouri in the Early Eighteenth Century* (Volume 94 in the prestigious Civilization of the American Indian Series). Hotz's book is the product of a remarkable feat of ethnological detection that has added to and encouraged the study of Indian, Spanish, and international intrigue in eighteenth-century western America.

Hotz concluded that the paintings depicted two New Mexican expeditions. Segesser I, he wrote, portrays mounted Indian auxiliaries with Spanish weapons attacking a tipi village defended by Indians on foot. He theorized that the painting recorded a punitive mission led by Valverde. Segesser II, he continued, shows Spanish and Pueblo troops surrounded by other European soldiers and naked Indians. Hotz recognized the battle as the ambush of the Pedro de Villasur expedition and even identified Villasur, Father Mínguez, José Domínguez (Villasur's chief aid), Joseph Naranjo, and Jean L'Archévèque, as well as the battle's location.

For the most part, subsequent research has verified and amplified Hotz's conclusions. However, the precise expedition depicted in Segesser I has become the subject of speculation. The painting could represent any of the numerous Spanish expeditions to punish Plains Indians. Beginning with Vargas's reentry into New Mexico in 1692, every New Mexican expedition included Spanish soldiers and Indian allies, as shown in the painting. In Segesser II, Frenchmen and Indians attack a hopelessly outnumbered Spanish contingent, bolstering Valverde's explanation of the Villasur calamity.

Most but not all scholars believe the creators of the paintings were probably Spanish-trained artists in New Mexico who worked from eyewitness descriptions. Both paintings have ornate baroque borders, indicating European influence. One recent theory is that the paintings were commissioned to adorn the home of some wealthy military man living on the northern frontier. Current research suggests that the Juan Bautista de Anza family of Sonora may have been the first owners.

The story of the Segesser paintings came full circle in 1984. Acting on information supplied by the Joslyn Art Museum in Omaha and the University of Nebraska State Museum, the Palace of the Governors staff began corresponding with the paintings' owner, Dr. André von Segesser (Fig. 6.5).[18] These individuals felt that the Palace of the

Cup-hilt broadsword (espada anch) of the type depicted in the
hide painting referred to as Segesser I. Segesser File, courtesy of
the Museum of New Mexico, Palace of the Governors.
Negative number 147832.

Governors in Santa Fe would be the most logical repository for the
Segesser paintings. A brief look at the subject matter of the paintings
explains this viewpoint. Segesser II includes contemporary drawings
of royal presidio troops who were stationed at the Palace. Those men,
Spanish as well as Pueblo Indians, are ancestors of many New Mexicans today. The staff became committed to bringing these rare and
important statements of southwestern colonial history to Santa Fe.

Dr. Segesser was pleased to hear of the Palace staff's interest. He,
too, felt that the paintings should come to New Mexico. Before
arrangements could be made, however, a number of questions had to
be answered: Could the paintings withstand travel? How would they
be affected by the climate of New Mexico? What would their true mon-
etary value be? To answer these questions, the Museum of New Mexico Foundation sent me to Zürich to inspect the paintings. On 11
February 1985, I examined them at Sotheby's in Zürich with Dr. Segesser and a number of experts, who tested the paintings to determine
their authenticity and durability. The consensus was that the paintings could and should travel to New Mexico.[19] This conclusion was
reaffirmed on a subsequent trip to Lucerne, Switzerland, where representatives of the Palace met with Dr. Segesser.

With these assurances, the Museum of New Mexico requested an
eighteen-month loan of the Segesser paintings. While in Santa Fe, the
paintings could be properly inspected by the museum's conservation
staff, exhibited at the Palace, and officially appraised. It was hoped
that the presence of the intriguing works would generate enough local

Thomas E. Chávez, Dr. André von Segesser, and Charles Bennett,
Santa Fe, Summer 1988. Segesser File, courtesy of the Museum of
New Mexico, Palace of the Governors, Santa Fe.

support to raise funds to purchase them for the Palace of the Governors. Dr. Segesser agreed to the proposed plan. On 11 March 1986,
after a trip strewn with delays, the paintings arrived at the Palace of
the Governors. The next day, members of the media were invited to
witness the removal of the paintings from the crate and to participate
in the first viewing of them on the North American continent in more
than two centuries (Fig. 6.7).[20]

Since their arrival, the paintings have evoked much interest.
Scholars from as far away as the Vatican have come to the Palace of
the Governors to see them. With funding from the New Mexico Endow-
ment for the Humanities, the Palace staff organized and hosted a symposium on the paintings for historians, anthropologists, and art
historians. The public is now enjoying these valuable documents of

Borderlands history; they are truly a window through which we can view a part of the Southwest's cultural heritage.

Art and Artifacts

Segesser I measures 13½ by 4½ feet; Segesser II measures 17 by 4½ feet. The third of the original three paintings has not been located. Both surviving paintings consist of bison or elk hides, cut into rectangles, tanned and smoked, and stitched together with sinew to form long surfaces. They show signs of wear, which is to be expected at their great age. Pieces are missing from both, and the natural pigments used to paint them have faded.

The bright and original "curiosities" from the New World were apparently heavily used by the Segesser family, probably as tapestries or wall decorations. Nail holes are evident around the borders of the hides. Sharper colors on the border of Segesser I indicate that a frame, probably of wood, once surrounded it. The backs of both paintings once received coats of glue. A rectangular piece cut from the lower left side of Segesser I apparently was removed to fit the painting around a door or window frame. This alteration may have been done in the nineteenth century, when the painting probably hung in the Huenenberg Castle, a Segesser family home near Ebikon, Switzerland. Family tradition indicates that the painting hung on a second-floor wall, the measurements of which match the cutout.[21] Also inexplicably missing are border pieces in the upper left and on the extreme right.

A fourth section missing from Segesser I may someday be recovered. This piece, which measures about thirty inches across, includes a painting of an Indian tepee village. According to Hotz, the section was cut out and given to a painter named Benz by Heinrich Viktor von Segesser-Crivelli, who owned the paintings from 1890 to 1894. Sometime before 1908, Benz sold the section to an architect named August am Rhyn, who still had the piece in 1960.[22]

Segesser II is by far the more complete of the two paintings. Only one piece on its extreme right is missing. In 1976, when the painting was photographed for a Time-Life publication, it still included this section, which depicts a Pueblo Indian auxiliary who is facing right (apparently guarding the horse herd during the attack).[23]

Detail of Segesser II. The blue-robed Franciscan Fray Juan
Mínguez, in the center of this section, is clutching a crucifix
and running toward the besieged New Mexicans to administer last rites. Behind him is Joseph Naranjo, chief war-
captain of all Pueblo auxiliary troops. Notice the cruciform
stirrup of the Spanish soldier on horseback who is
fearlessly charging the enemy. Courtesy of the Museum
of New Mexico, Palace of the Governors.

Cruciform wrought iron stirrup as depicted in Segesser II.
Courtesy of the Museum of New Mexico,
Palace of the Governors. Negative number 147833.

The Segesser hide paintings are particularly valuable to us today because early pictorial representations of historical events in the present-day United States are extremely rare. Such visual records are especially scarce in the Southwest, although we do have a few examples. Some of the early cartographic works show Indians as well as native flora and fauna. A seventeenth-century manuscript drawing depicts an event that occurred in Sonoyta, Sonora. In 1693, Father

Adam Gilg, S.J., drew a strolling family of Seri Indians, again in Sonora. Various late eighteenth-century Spanish chroniclers illustrated their reports, and numerous illustrations of *mestizaje*, or people of various blood mixtures, have been discovered.[24] Some southwestern Indian pictographs, notably those at the Painted Cave in Bandelier National Monument thirty miles west of Santa Fe, show Spaniards riding horseback and wearing flat, wide-brimmed hats similar to the ones that appear in Segesser II.

However, no visual record can match the Segesser paintings in size and detail. They have been used as historical documents to extract previously unknown information. The Segesser paintings are reminiscent of early Spanish colonial codices done in the sixteenth century under the tutelage of priests, most notably Fray Bernardino de Sahagún. He used Indian artists to document testimony from tribal elders. This type of manuscript art flourished until around 1660; Techialoyan manuscript paintings of various Mexican villages were still being done from 1700 to 1743.[25]

Despite the relatively late date of the Segesser paintings, they bear some similarities to manuscript art. They are historical documents that may have been intended to accompany written reports. It is possible that like Sahagún's *Codex Florentino*, which was made to be sent to the Spanish King and the Council of the Indies, the Segesser renditions were created for government officials, in which case they would have been painted to administrative specifications.[26] The style of the paintings, especially of Segesser I, is reminiscent of some of the postconquest codices (sixteenth-century fold-out books) or *lienzos* (large cloth paintings executed by Indian artists under the tutelage of Spanish priests).

Other early pictorial representations of American colonial life do exist. There are several images of life in the eastern United States in the pictorial scenes of artists John White (works dated 1584–87) and Jacques Le Moyne (1564). These were reproduced by Dutch engraver Théodore de Bry, who also illustrated Sir Francis Drake's meeting with Indians in Alta California.[27] However, many scholars feel that in size and detail the recently rediscovered Segesser paintings are as noteworthy as any other colonial pictorial representations.

Continuing Odyssey

On 31 October 1988, the Segesser paintings officially became the property of the State of New Mexico. Between the time of their return to New Mexico and the final payment, much had been accomplished to keep them "home" as well as to unravel their history and the history they illustrate. The state legislature appropriated money for their acquisition in 1988. A check was given to Dr. Segesser, and the dream of the paintings' purchase became reality.[28]

Subsequent research has identified the ship *Nuestra Señora del Rosario* — alias the *Alcón*, or *Falcon* — as the vessel that transported Segesser's goods, which included semiprecious stones and a paper model of a church, to Europe. The ship, captained by Domingo Apodaca, sailed from Vera Cruz to Cádiz in southern Spain. After a stop at Havana, the *Falcon* arrived in Cádiz on 29 December 1760. Almost three months later, the ship's owner, Tomás Apodaca, received Segesser's "regales."[29]

The third painting is still missing, but researchers are investigating two possibilities. The first is that Domingo Apodaca kept one of the paintings as a curiosity for his own collection and that the painting, like the other two, has been handed down from generation to generation. Unfortunately, no Apodacas currently reside in Cádiz, although the main street of the city is named Avenida Apodaca. According to local tradition, the family has moved to the Jérez country in southern Andalusia. A survey of Cádiz's museums and cultural affairs office has not turned up any information.

A second possibility is that the third painting survived in Switzerland. A colleague and friend of Father Segesser's in Sonora was Father Antonio Balthasar. The Balthasars are still a prominent Swiss family and may have the third painting, packed away and forgotten. Another possibility is that the painting no longer exists or has been cut into pieces and dispersed, which is what was beginning to happen to Segesser I. Dr. Louis Balthasar was enlisted to check on the possibility that someone in his family might know about the third painting. Balthasar wrote to relatives and checked the "family chronicles" but found nothing. One family source, according to Dr. Balthasar, would have been of help, but he "died as a Cardinal to the Pope [at the] end of May this year [1988]."[30]

The staff of the Palace of the Governors continues to search for the pieces missing from the two existing paintings. Photographs exist of two of the pieces missing from the Segesser paintings, and the staff knows of at least two others.[31] The largest, which the Palace of the Governors staff reproduced from a photograph for the Segesser exhibition, depicts a tipi Indian village. The piece recently surfaced in Basel, Switzerland, where it was sold to the Segesser Family Trust. Upon hearing this news I flew to Lucerne, Switzerland, to meet with Dr. André von Segesser and the trust's representative, Dr. Ludwig von Segesser, about the possibility of acquiring the piece. At this point, the trust has decided to hold on to the section and to store it in a bank vault in Lucerne.[32]

So the odyssey of the Segesser paintings continues. The paintings have been returned to New Mexico and are exhibited in the Palace of the Governors, but they are not complete. Perhaps the missing pieces and the third painting will be discovered and returned. Meanwhile, the public has become interested in viewing and studying these unique pieces of early American history (the paintings have become the major request for group tours at the museum), and a number of scholars have visited Santa Fe specifically to undertake research on the paintings. Future plans call for a traveling exhibition in the United States and Europe and publication of an anthology of articles dealing with the paintings. All can learn from the history contained in these paintings and appreciate their beauty.

Notes

The success of this project has required a combined effort of many people. New Mexico State Senator Les Houston and State Representative Max Coll initiated and guided the legislation that provided the acquisition money. Santa Feans Howard and Meriom Kastner helped with negotiations. Howard translated all our correspondence into German and all the Swiss correspondence into English. Jeffrey Hengesbaugh championed the paintings enough to get the politicians interested and involved. Fabian Chávez was our unofficial lobbyist. Garrey Carruthers, the governor of New Mexico, supported the state's acquisition of the paintings. Dr. Renata Wente-Lucas, curator of the Ledermuseum in Offenbaugh, West Germany; Dr. Günter Gall, director to the Ledermuseum; and Hans Kelker, a chemist from the Hoechst Company in Frankfurt investigated the paintings when they were in Zurich. In Nebraska, Marsha Gallagher of the Joslyn Museum and Dr. James Gunnerson of the University of Nebraska State Museum first made us aware of the paintings' availability. The staff at the Nebraska State Historical Society provided letters of support and were very informative. Mark Chávez provided some timely and helpful publicity ideas that were instrumental in acquiring the paintings. Charles Bennett, assistant director at the Palace of the Governors, has been an equal partner in this project. We thank these people and the many who wrote letters, spread the word verbally and contributed in excess of $60,000 toward the travel, exhibition, and conservation of the paintings.

1. Gottfried Hotz, *Indian Skin Paintings from the American Southwest* (Norman: University of Oklahoma Press, 1970), pp. 8-11.

2. John Francis Bannon, *The Spanish Borderlands Frontier, 1513-1821* (New York: Rinehart and Winston, 1970), p. 97; and Fray Angélico Chávez, *Origins of New Mexico Families in the Spanish Colonial Period* (Albuquerque: The University of New Mexico Press, 1973), p. 129.

3. Guillaume Delisle, "Carte du Mexique et de la Floride des Terres Angloises . . . ," Paris, 1703 (original); "Carte d'Amerique drefsée pour l'usage du Roy," Paris, 1722 (original); "Carte de la Louisiane et Cours du Mississippi . . . ," Paris, 1718 (photocopy). All maps are in the History Library, Palace of the Governors (PG), Santa Fe.

4. Bannon, *Spanish Borderlands Frontier*, p. 127; and map, "Le Nouveau Mexique, Appelé aussi Nouvelle Grenade et Marata, avec partie de Californie," 1686-88, Vicenzo Maria Coronelli, History Library, PG.

5. Alfred B. Thomas, *After Coronado: Spanish Exploration Northeast of New Mexico, 1696-1727* (Norman: University of Oklahoma Press, 1935), p. 13.

6. Hotz, *Skin Paintings*, p. 176.

7. Bannon, *Spanish Borderlands Frontier*, pp. 128-29.

8. Fray Angélico Chávez, "Pohe-Yemo's Representative and the Pueblo Revolt of 1680," *New Mexico Historical Review* 42 (April 1967): 109; "Testimony on behalf of Antonio Valverde y Cosío," May 27–June 3, 1720, No. 308, Spanish Archives of New Mexico (SANM), frames 1016-18, State Records Center and Archives, Santa Fe; "Diary of the Campaign of Juan Páez Hurtado, 1715," in Thomas, *After Coronado*, pp. 94-98.

9. Thomas, *After Coronado*, p. 128.

10. "Diary of the Campaign Led by Governor Valverde, 1719," as translated in Thomas, *After Coronado*, pp. 110-33.

11. Bannon, *Spanish Borderlands Frontier*, p. 129; Hotz, *Skin Paintings*, p. 182; and "Testimony on behalf of Valverde," no. 308, SANM.

12. One source states that Father Mínguez was taken alive by the Indians and held prisoner in their village. There he was asked to show the Indians how to ride a horse; however, as soon as he mounted the animal, he sped away and escaped. Whether or not this story is true, Father Mínguez never made it back to New Mexico. See Henri Folmer, "Contraband Trade Between Louisiana and New Mexico in the Eighteenth Century," *New Mexico Historical Review* 16 (July 1941): 258. In reference to the Pawnees' involvement in the ambush there is Hotz's research (*Skin Paintings*, passim), the testimony of the survivors who referred to their attackers as "Pananas," and a symposium held in Santa Fe 7–8 August 1986 that included many ethnohistorians, none of whom disputed the presence of Pawnees (Segesser File, Palace of the Governors).

13. Félix Martínez to Viceroy Valero, 1720, quoted in Hotz, *Skin Paintings*, p. 204.

14. Order of Juan de Olivan Revolledo, 28 May 1727, no. 1728, SANM, role 6, frames 497-99.

15. Father Philipp von Segesser von Brunegg to Ulrich Franz Josef von Segesser, 11 April 1761, as quoted in Hotz, *Skin Paintings*, p. 9.

16. "Palace of the Governors: Report on the Segesser Paintings," p. 1, History Library, PG; E. Boyd to Gottfried Hotz, 1960, as quoted in Hotz, *Skin Paintings*, pp. 227-28; E. Boyd to Dr. Savoie Lottinville, 15 March 1961, copy of correspondence in Segesser File, PG.

17. Oliver LaFarge to Gottfried Hotz, 20 November 1959 and Jane Ivancovich to E. Boyd, 3 November 1959, Segesser File, PG.

18. "Segesser Report," p. 2.

19. Dr. Günter Gall to Dr. Thomas Chávez, 9 July 1985, "Segesser Report," pp. 34-38.

20. *Santa Fe Reporter*, 12 March 1986; *Albuquerque Tribune*, 12 March 1986; *New Mexican*, 13 March and 9 April 1986.

21. Hotz, *Skin Paintings*, pp. 11-12.

22. Ibid., plate 3 and p. 11.

23. *The Spanish West* (New York: Time-Life, 1976), pp. 72-73.

24. For examples, see Richard Polese, ed., *The Malaspina Expedition: "In the Pursuit of Knowledge . . ."* (Santa Fe: Museum of New Mexico Press, 1977); *El Mestizaje Americano*, ed. Concepción García Sáiz (Madrid: Museo de América, 1986); and Pedro Alonso O'Crouly, *A Description of the Kingdom of New Spain*, trans. Sean Galvin (1774; rpt. San Francisco: John Howell Books, 1972).

25. Donald Robertson, *Mexican Manuscript Painting of the Early Colonial Period: The Metropolitan Schools* (New Haven: Yale University Press, 1959), pp. 3, 30-31, 37, 47, 55; Donald Robertson, "Techialoyan Manuscripts and Paintings with a Catalogue," *Handbook of Middle American Indians*, Vol. 14 (Austin: University of Texas Press, 1975), pp. 262-64.

26. Robertson, *Mexican Manuscript Painting*, pp. 9, 15.

27. Dr. Bernard Fontana to Dr. Thomas Chávez, 31 March 1986, Segesser File.

28. The appropriation is contained in General Appropriation of the Legislature of the State of New Mexico, 38th Legislature, 2nd session, Laws 1988, Chapter 13, page 174 (copy in the Palace of the Governors).

29. Register of Nuestra Señora del Rosario, 1760; and Duplicado del Navio nombrado Nuestra Señora. . . , 1760, and Sr. Con.[dor] Princ.[pal] de la R[l] Casa de Contratación, folio 40, 30 March 1761, Contratación 2564, Archivo General de Indias. Segesser's mailing is listed as "Regales de Caxon. . . ," gifts in a trunk, with a drawing of the Segesser family coat of arms in the margin.

30. Dr. Georg von Segesser to Dr. Thomas Chávez, 26 May 1988; Chávez to Dr. Louis Balthasar, 18 October 1988; Balthasar to Chávez, 23 November 1988, folder 1, box V, Segesser File. This correspondence does raise the possibility that the Vatican Museum may have the painting.

31. The missing endpiece of Segesser II is published in color in *The Spanish West* (1976), p. 73. The original negative is now in possession of the Palace of the Governors. One of the pieces in Segesser I was published in Hotz, *Skin Paintings*, (1970), plate 3.

32. Hotz, *Skin Paintings*, plate 3 and p. 11; André von Segesser to Dr. Thomas Chávez, 31 October 1988; Chávez to Dr. Ludwig von Segesser, 23 February 1989; Ludwig von Segesser to Chávez, 16 March 1989; and André von Segesser to Chávez, 4 April 1989. The meeting took place on Sunday, 5 February 1989, at the Segesser family home in Lucerne.

✝

7

The Genízaro Experience in Spanish New Mexico

Russell M. Magnaghi

The colonial period in American history includes not only the English experience on the Atlantic shore but also the Spanish story in the Southwest and the approaches to the Great Plains.[1] Part of the New Mexican story is the emergence of a new people who became part of our multicultural heritage, the detribalized Indians, who were given the name genízaros and were eventually absorbed into Pueblo-Spanish society.[2] The Spanish tried to implement their Indian policy on the Great Plains; however, frustrated by the environment and the native people, they remained in their New Mexican settlements and watched as Plains Indians involuntarily came to them.

Indian Slaves and Servants

The Spanish policy on Indian slavery helped determine the character of Indian relations along the New Mexican frontier. Between 1503 and 1510 the Spanish crown authorized the enslavement of Caribbean Indians who practiced cannibalism, engaged in warfare, or rebelled against the Spanish. A royal decree dated 17 November 1526 instructed Spanish explorers to read the *Requerimiento* (Requirement) to Indians they encountered in all new territories. If the Indians did not submit, the resulting warfare was considered just, and the Indians could be enslaved. The New Laws of 1542 prohibited the enslavement

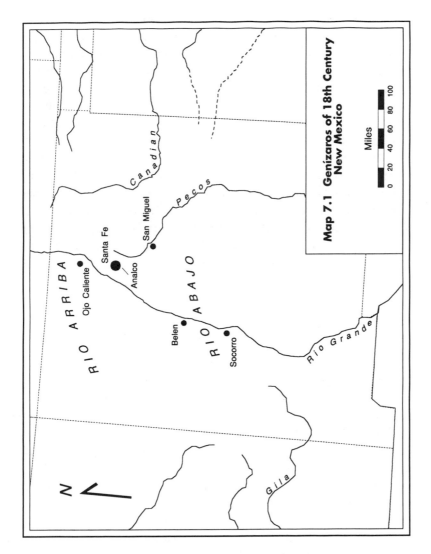

Genízaros in Eighteenth-Century New Mexico.

of Indians, but these were frequently ignored. Ultimately the "just war" concept provided the mechanism whereby non-Christian Indians were enslaved.[3] The Spanish carried this concept and practice with them after they left the valley of Mexico and marched northward.

When Francisco Vázquez de Coronado's men reached the Great Plains in the 1540s, they found an inhospitable environment. The Plains Apaches dominated the area from the sandhills of present-day Nebraska to the Pecos River in West Texas until the close of the seventeenth century.[4] These nomadic people disappointed the Spanish, who were seeking stable and cohesive communities of Indians upon whom their institutions could be imposed. Moreover, many of the Spanish governors who went to New Mexico after the beginning of settlement in 1598 were ineffective leaders who regarded their appointments as opportunities for personal gain.[5] As a result, the Spanish exploited the Pueblo Indians and often attacked and enslaved the Plains Apaches, whom they perceived as uncivilized. These Indian captives were one of the Plains' few profitable commodities, being sent south to the labor-starved silver mines of Nueva Vizcaya.[6]

Trade in Indian Captives

The relationship between the Spanish and the Indians was further altered with the Pueblo Revolt of 1680 and the promulgation of the colonial legal code known as the *Recopilacíon* of 1681. The Pueblo Revolt rendered the Spanish reluctant to enslave or exploit the Indians of the Southwest. The *Recopilacíon* carefully spelled out the Christian obligation to ransom captive Indians enslaved by other Indian nations. This principle was given further royal sanction in 1694 after a group of Navajos killed their Pawnee captives in front of the Spaniards, who refused to ransom them.[7]

As these policy changes were being institutionalized in the early eighteenth century, the Comanches migrated from their homes in present north central Colorado to the southern Plains. They proceeded to drive off the Utes and Plains Apaches, and by midcentury they dominated the Plains with French firearms and ammunition readily available through Wichita brokers. In their encounters with Plains Apaches and later with Comanches, the poorly equipped and undermanned Spaniards found that the Indians acted individually and would not enter into peace negotiations as a political entity. As a result, both Indian and Spanish settlements of New Mexico came under constant attack.[8]

The Spanish duty to ransom any and all captives who entered New Mexico quickly created a market for Comanche prisoners, not only among Spanish and Pueblo people but also among Plains Indians who stood in the way of Comanche expansion. The trade in captives took place at traditional Indian fair sites such as Taos and Pecos. In 1744 Fray Miguel Menchero observed that Taos's importance lay in the fact that non-Christian Indians entered the pueblo to sell captives. These were such an important commodity that Fray Pedro Serrano referred to them as the "gold and silver and richest treasures for the governor." Prices varied according to the sex and age of the captive. In 1776 a female Indian between twelve and twenty years old was exchanged for either two good horses and trifles or a mule and a scarlet cover. Males were worth half as much as females.[9]

The Plains Indians who were introduced into New Mexico as slaves came from tribes throughout the region: Plains Apache, Comanche, Jumano, Kiowa, Pawnee, and Wichita. The Pawnees were commonly taken as slaves throughout the colonial era and were found in both French and Spanish communities on the eastern and western edges of the Plains, respectively. The Jumanos and Pawnees began interacting with the Spanish in the seventeenth century, although their baptismal entries begin in 1702–03. The Kiowas begin to show in the records in the late 1720s, and the Comanches are first listed in the Spanish records in the early eighteenth century. A final group of Plains Indians who first appear in the Spanish church records in 1742 are the "A" or "Aa" Indians. Although scholars have thought they were Skidi Pawnees, Dolores Gunnerson has identified them as Crows.[10]

The First Genízaros

The captives who remained in New Mexico were divided into two groups, *indios sirvientes* (Indian servants) and *indios genízaros*. Indian servants were non-Christian Indians who were allotted to the settlers after having been ransomed at the fairs. According to the *Recopilación*, it was the duty of the Spanish owner to acculturate them; the servants' duty was to work off their ransom payment.[11] The process of acculturation began immediately and was expected to be thorough enough to place these Indians within the hierarchy of Spanish society. Through baptism they entered the Catholic faith and received Christian names. Being of unknown parentage, these Indians were listed in baptismal records as "of the house of," "servant of," or "adopted by." Their surnames were taken from the households they were attached to or from their godparents.[12]

As part of the indoctrination process these Indians learned a simple form of Spanish. Fray Francisco Atanasio Domínguez noted in 1776 that genízaros were not very fluent in Spanish and added that he did not believe they would become so even with practice.[13] Nonetheless, because they originated from diverse tribes with varied languages, the genízaros adopted Spanish as their lingua franca. They had no hope of returning to their own people, so these unfortunate Indians were forced to acculturate into Spanish society. They mixed European values with their own, dressed in Spanish clothes, and followed the customs of the dominant society.

The practice of keeping Indian servants under even these circumstances frequently led to abuses among the Spanish. In 1763 two female genízaras appealed directly to Governor Tomás Vélez Cachupín, complaining that they had been improperly cared for and not instructed in the Christian faith. Furthermore, they had been sent out to tend sheep, which was considered a male occupation, and as a consequence one of them had been raped. The governor removed them from their masters and placed them in homes "where they might be instructed in Christian doctrine and customs, and be fed and clothed through household chores appropriate to their sex."[14] Large numbers of servants did not receive proper treatment and fled the settlements, and many lived as "apostates" with the Apaches in the mountains. In an effort to remedy abuses, the provincial government intervened and removed Indians from their masters if mistreatment could be proved.[15]

Once Indian servants had paid their debts, they were free to leave the Spanish household and became known as genízaros. Although a number of meanings have been given to this term over the years, Fray Agustín Morfí gave a precise and correct definition in 1779: "This name is given to the children of the captives of different [Indian] nations who have married in the province."[16] The term was used through the eighteenth and into the early nineteenth centuries. Known by the New Mexicans as "children of the enemy," genízaros lacked social status because they were neither Spanish nor Indian. As a result, they could not be admitted into the pueblos, nor could they legally obtain land. As Fray Damian Martínez wrote in 1792, they were reduced to living without "land, cattle or other property with which to make a living except their bows and arrows."[17]

Genízaros in Frontier Outposts

At first the genízaros naturally congregated in the barrio of Analco in the southern section of Santa Fe; others sought acceptance in Pueblo villages. Their lack of legal status and the increased population pressure on land in the Río Grande Valley made their settlement difficult.[18] At the same time, however, raids by Plains Indians — Apaches and Comanches — and by Navajos and Utes made it imperative that the frontier regions be settled for defense. Many genízaros were therefore relocated in outlying districts to serve as buffers for the Spanish settlements.[19]

In the Río Abajo region (south from La Bajada and Cochití Pueblo), Belén was settled early by the genízaros. By 1740 they were protesting attempts by the local *alcalde mayor* to seize their lands, and by 1790 they were living throughout the community but were concentrated in Plaza Number Three, called Nuestra Señora de los Dolores de los Genízaros.[20] By the late eighteenth century the settlement contained a large, varied population and was raised to the status of a district. The pueblos of Valencia and Cerro de Tomé, located thirty leagues to the south of Santa Fe, were established by Governor Gáspar Domingo de Mendoza in 1740 after forty families of genízaros applied to be resettled there. They farmed and scouted, defending the frontier with bravery and diligence. By the mid-1770s there was a community of Apache genízaros at the mission of Socorro near El Paso. San Miguel del Vado, east of the Sangre de Cristo Mountains and Pecos, was originally settled in 1794 as a frontier outpost against Plains Indians. It was constructed for defense, with its plaza surrounded by houses and a church. Genízaro soldier-farmers were its first residents, but after 1799 they were joined by mestizos and other genízaros who were seeking arable land. Eventually a few pacified Comanches and some Pueblo Indians from Nambé joined the population.[21]

In the Río Arriba region to the north of Santa Fe, other genízaro settlements began to appear. Ojo Caliente, in the direct path of Indian raiders, was created by order of Governor Joachim Codallos y Rabál in an attempt to halt Comanche and Ute incursions. However, the danger of attack was so great that even the tenacious genízaros who formed the majority of the population were forced to abandon the community. San Tomás de Abiquiú was established in 1748, and by 1752 Governor Vélez Cachupín noted that there were 108 genízaros living thoro, with 39 men hearing arms. A later governor, Fermín de Mendinueta, sought to place genízaros without fixed residences throughout the Río Puerco region to assist in the reestablishment of San Miguel de Carnue in the Sandía Mountains. The settlement had been founded in 1763 to help curb Apache raids into the Albuquerque region but was abandoned in 1771. In order to attract genízaros to the enterprise, colonial administrators promised to put them on an equal footing with Spanish settlers, but continued Apache raids forced the governor to abandon resettlement plans.[22]

Genízaro Population

Data on the genízaro population are incomplete, and available information must be adjusted to include servants who were in the process of becoming genízaros. The 1750 census of New Mexico showed a genízaro population of 154 and a servant population of 693; combined, the two populations constituted 13.2 percent of the colony's total residents. Within Albuquerque alone this combination made up 28.7 percent of the total. In 1758 Bernardo de Miera y Pacheco noted that the population was divided into Spanish and genízaro portions. Of the latter he noted that there were 58 heads of families and 225 individuals. An anonymous report written in 1765 indicated that there were 191 genízaro families and 677 individuals living in New Mexico. By 1776 42 genízaro families totaling 164 individuals, or 12.25 percent of the population of Santa Fe, lived in the barrio of Analco, where they had their own church. Genízaros not only resided in their own communities or in barrios like Analco but were scattered in Pueblo villages as well; in 1790 they could be found at Taos, San Juan, Santa Clara, and Nambé. Although the genízaros often came from warring tribes and, according to Spanish observers, would have been enemies in their native state, they lived together in peace in New Mexico.[23]

Throughout Spain's American colonies there was great emphasis placed upon racial classification.[24] New Mexico's population was divided in the 1790 census into to the following ethnic derivations:

Spanish, Indian, mestizo (generally understood to be a mixture of Spanish and Mexican Indian), coyote (a mixture of Spanish and of New Mexican Indian), mulatto (sometimes used with its usual connotation and sometimes used by the friars to indicate a mixture of Spanish and Indian), genízaro, *color quebrado* (literally "broken color," probably denoting any combination of white, Indian, and black ancestry), and *lobo* (racial mixture). The population was "whitened" by upward economic mobility and marriage between intermediate groups. Children took the status of the mother. Intermarriage tended to dissolve the so-called castes, especially on the frontier, yet it simultaneously motivated increased exclusivism at the upper end of New Mexican societies. The 1790 census shows that genízaro males were married to women of varied racial origin: mestiza (24), genízara (11), Indian (9), coyote (3), and color quebrado, Spanish, and mulatta (2 each). Two genízara women married Pueblo Indians from Soccoro near El Paso; the men moved into their wives' community at Belén, where racial mixture was tolerated.[25]

Genízaro Occupations

The genízaros' occupations changed with their status. The first genízaros were referred to in the Spanish records as the "servants" — but never as the "slaves" — of the Spaniards who had ransomed them. Those who were released from their debt were usually forced into menial tasks and were considered the poorest residents of the community. Later some became skilled basketmakers, potters, and shield designers.[26] In 1776 Fray Francisco Domínguez critically evaluated the role of the genízaros he encountered on his tour of New Mexico. He did not note the occupations of those he met in Santa Fe but recorded finding many servants in other Spanish communities and ranches. Some genízaros at Abiquiú were starving in the midst of good farmland, but to the south, at Los Jarales, they were farming small plots of arable land.[27] By 1790 most genízaros were farmers (28.6 percent) and day laborers (25 percent), occupations characteristic of the local economy. Weaving woolen blankets and cloth for coats, serge, serapes, baize, sackcloth, carpeting, and stockings was a common cottage industry throughout the province, where sheep were plentiful and fabrics were considered a medium of exchange. As a result, 15.3 percent of the genízaro work force found employment as carders, spinners, and weavers. The remainder were occupied as muleteers, carpenters, shoe-makers, builders, sweepers, and shepherds.[28]

Because they lived in frontier settlements, many genízaros became traders with Indians during periods of peace. At Abiquiú Ute Indians arrived in late October or early November to trade deerskins for horses and broad knives (*belduques*) and jerked deer and buffalo meat for corn flour at the annual trade fair. There was also a small trade in captive children.[29] After the Anza-Ecueracapa treaty of 1786 (one of several peace accords Governor Juan Bautista de Anza brought about with the Comanches, Utes, and Navajos), the "indigent and rude classes of the frontier villages," known as *comancheros*, could venture onto the Plains to trade with the Comanches. Many of the genízaros knew Plains Indian languages, and with a very small investment in "a few trinkets and trumperies of all kinds, and perhaps a bag of bread and maybe another of *pinole*," they might barter for a mule or two.[30] Spanish and Mexican officials promoted such trade to maintain knowledge of the territory, the Indians, and European intrusion.

The Spanish had inadequate military forces and finances for guarding the New Mexican frontier and relied on Indian auxiliaries, both Pueblos and genízaros, who outfitted expeditions with their own resources. Genízaro military equipment was basic because the Spanish did not supply them with arms. In the late 1750s sixty-three genízaros in the province were armed with the traditional bow and arrow and eleven possessed lances, but only three had muskets.[31] The Spanish hoped that genízaro farmer-soldiers would stop Apache, Comanche, and Ute raids, and in many cases they acted with bravery and zeal. Genízaro troops participated in offensive operations as well, attacking their traditional enemies — the people who had enslaved them — and halting, at least temporarily, the constant raids against New Mexican settlements. Although pay was nonexistent, the genízaros took such booty as captives, horses, livestock, and food-stuffs.[32]

The genízaros were effective frontier warriors. During the summer of 1777, fifty-five genízaros successfully fought the White Mountain Apaches. Their reputation grew with their successes, and at times local commanders specifically requested their presence on a military mission. An official genízaro fighting force was organized in 1808 when the governor created the *tropa de genízaro*, commanded by a corporal from their own ranks; unfortunately, the history of this unit has been lost.[33] Genízaros' fluency in Plains Indian languages made them

excellent scouts and interpreters. In 1776 at Ranchos de Taos the Indians spoke Spanish, the Taos language, and "to a considerable extent
the Comanche, Ute and Apache languages."[34] When Josef Miguel led
an expedition from New Mexico to the Missouri River in the summer
of 1800, he took along four genízaro interpreters.[35] Although individual genízaros were trusted as scouts or interpreters, as a group they
were regarded as potentially traitorous, and on a number of occasions
some of them were tried for sedition.[36]

Through economic mobility and intermarriage with mestizos,
genízaros were able to enter Spanish society, and some played leadership roles. At El Paso in 1765, ten genízaro families had acquired the
status of citizens. When the genízaro-dominated barrio of Analco at
Santa Fe was threatened with destruction, Ventura Bustamente, a
genízaro, traveled to Arizpe in 1780 to protest this action.[37] Other
genízaros played important roles in the religious life of the communities. In 1812 José Cristóbal Guerro, a San Miguel del Vado genízaro of
Comanche extraction, led a drive for a resident priest. His petition to
the bishop of Durango had so many names on it that the bishop
thought the town would become one of the most populous in New Mexico. The lack of secular priests in the late eighteenth century caused
many Spanish and genízaro communities to turn to penitential confra-
ternities (*cofradías*) to administer religious affairs. This movement
continues with certain modifications into the present century.[38]

Although some genízaros found occupations and status within
Hispanic society, many others stayed at the bottom of the social lad-
der. Court records show that genízaros often were common thieves,
stealing horses and livestock and cheating Indians at trade fairs.
Some were picked up as vagabonds as far south as Chihuahua and
returned to New Mexico. Others spent their time gambling and engag-
ing in petty crimes. In one instance a genízaro and his wife allegedly
killed Fray Ordoñez y Machado, the parish priest at Abiquiú, by
witchcraft.[39]

Americans and Assimilation

In the nineteenth century Mexican independence and the arrival
of Americans down the Santa Fe Trail gradually erased the distinction
between genízaro and Spaniard. The Plan of Iguala, which preceded
Mexican independence in 1821, stated that the government was no

longer concerned with the racial origins of its citizens. After independence the central government exerted little influence in New Mexico; the genízaros coexisted with their Spanish and Pueblo neighbors but continued to be viewed as a different element within provincial society.

When Americans first went to New Mexico they were unfamiliar with the local social traditions and in many instances were unable to make a clear distinction between Spaniards, Pueblo Indians, and genízaros. For example, when American trader Thomas James left San Miguel del Vado, primarily a genízaro community, in 1821, he wrote that he was joined by "the alcalde and a company of *Spaniards* bound for Santa Fe" (emphasis added). James repeatedly used the terms "Spaniards," "Spanish Indians," and "Mexican Indians" when he was probably referring to genízaros. More than a decade later Josiah Gregg noted that the population consisted of white creoles, "mestizos or mixed creoles," and Pueblo Indians. In his estimation, mestizos or mixed creoles accounted for 84.2 percent of New Mexico's seventy thousand residents. The genízaros would have fallen into this class.[40]

The genízaro population continued to follow earlier settlement patterns. They had already settled San Miguel del Vado, and early in the century they continued down the Pecos Valley and settled San José del Vado, La Cuesta, and, around 1822, Antón Chico, which remained the eastern gateway to New Mexico until the 1860s.[41] In these frontier locations the genízaros continued to play an active role with the Indians and the commerce of the Plains. Their employment as comancheros, interpreters, and hunters (*ciboleros*) continued until the 1870s. The frontier settlements of the genízaros also attracted some Comanche and Kiowa settlers, who provided an important link with the Comanche and possibly spared New Mexico the disastrous raids that befell Durango and Chihuahua to the south. With the development of the Santa Fe trade, genízaros joined the caravans and traveled to St. Louis and back as guides and interpreters. The demand for New Mexican–made blankets created opportunities for others in the weaving industry.[42]

The saga of José Ángel Gonzáles highlights the complexity of the assimilative process in New Mexico and illustrates the incomplete historical record. In August 1837 Hispanics and Pueblo Indians in Río Arriba rose in revolt and acclaimed Gonzáles governor. The new leader's origins were unclear. Was Gonzáles, a buffalo hunter from Taos, actually the son of a Pueblo mother and genízaro father and thus someone with close ties to the rebels? Or was he a Pueblo Indian from Taos or a *vecino* from Ranchos de Taos, as some sources indicate? When the insurrection was crushed after the battle of Pojoaque, Gonzáles and others were captured and executed. Although Governor Manuel Armijo called him a genízaro when he asked Padre Antonio Martínez to hear his final confession, the controversy over Gonzáles' origins cannot be settled by the existing primary sources. If he was a genízaro, he was the first and only person of his class to be governor of New Mexico.[43]

The genízaro people are unique in the history of Native Americans in the United States. By the time Anglo-Americans reached New Mexico, the genízaro people had been absorbed into Pueblo Indian life or into the lower social and economic strata of Hispanic society. The term "genízaro" fell into disuse and remains only in colonial documentation. Yet it has been estimated that by the late eighteenth century genízaros constituted one-third of the population of New Mexico.[44] They were an enduring human legacy of the cultural conflict on the Plains between Spaniards and the native population, Indians who became an integral part of Hispanic society in New Mexico and part of the American experience.

Notes

1. Two critical studies of Borderland historiography are Gerald E. Poyo and Gilberto M. Hinojosa, "Spanish Texas and Borderlands Historiography in Transition: Implications for United States History," *Journal of American History* 75 (September 1988): 393–416; and David J. Weber, "John Francis Bannon and the Historiography of the Spanish Borderlands," *Journal of the Southwest* 29 (Winter 1987): 331–63.

2. The term *genízaro* had its origins in Spain, where it designated a Spaniard of mixed European parentage. The contemporary spelling is *jenizaro,* meaning "one begotten by parents of different nations or composed of different species" or merely mixed, hybrid. The word is of Turkish origin *(yeni cerci* ,"new troops"). In English, *janizary* refers to Christian boys, primarily from Albania, Bulgaria, and Bosnia, who were seized by the Turks as annual tribute, instructed in the Muslim faith, and trained and enrolled as salaried infantry in the sultan's personal guard and in the main part of the army. Their discipline and loyalty made them one of the most formidable fighting forces in the fifteenth and sixteenth centuries.

They were eliminated in a series of reforms in 1826 (Fray Angélico Chávez, "Genízaros," *Handbook of North American Indians, Southwest* 9 [Washington, DC: Smithsonian Institution, 1979]: 198).

3. Charles Gibson, *Spain in America* (New York: Harper & Row, 1967), p. 38; Clarence H. Haring, *The Spanish Empire in America* (New York: Harcourt, Brace and World, 1947), p. 7; Russell M. Magnaghi, "The Indian Slave Trader: The Comanche, A Case Study" (Ph.D. diss., Saint Louis University, 1970), pp. 13–19.

4. Coronado to the King, 20 October 1541, in *The Coronado Expedition, 1540–1542, Annual Report of the Bureau of American Ethnology,* ed. George Winship (Washington, DC: Government Printing Office, 1896), pp. 364, 367–69. For a brief survey of Spanish intrusions onto the Great Plains, see Noel M. Loomis and Abraham P. Nasatir, *Pedro Vial and the Roads to Santa Fe* (Norman: University of Oklahoma Press, 1967), pp. 16–27; for the Plains Apache, see Karl H. Schlesier, "Rethinking the Dismal River Aspect and the Plains Athapaskans, A.D. 1692–1768," *Plains Anthropologist* 17 (May 1972): 101–33; and Michael B. Collins, "A Review of Llano Estacado Archaeology and Ethnohistory," *Plains Anthropologist* 16 (May 1971): 92–95.

5. France V. Scholes, *Church and State in New Mexico, 1610–1650* (Albuquerque: University of New Mexico Press, 1937), p. 70.

6. Philip W. Powell, *Soldiers, Indians and Silver: The Northward Advance of New Spain, 1550–1600* (Berkeley: University of California Press, 1952); Robert C. West, *The Mining Community in Northern New Spain: The Parral Mining District* (Berkeley: University of California Press, 1949), p. 52; Peter J. Bakewell in *Silver Mining and Society in Colonial Mexico: Zacatecas, 1546–1700* (Cambridge: Cambridge University Press, 1971), pp. 122–29, stresses the widespread use of free wage labor in and near Zacatecas rather than the use of Indian slaves.

7. *Recopilación de leyes de los reynos de las Indias. Mandadas imprimir y publicar por la Majestad católica del rey don Carlos II,* (Madrid, 1681), libro VII, título VII, leyes II and XVII; Alfred B. Thomas, ed., *After Coronado: Spanish Exploration Northeast of New Mexico, 1696–1727* (Norman: University of Oklahoma Press, 1935), pp. 13–14.

8. Catherine Price, "The Comanche Threat to Texas and New Mexico in the Eighteenth Century and the Development of Spanish Indian Policy," *Journal of the West* 24 (1985): 34–45. The classic work on Comanche life is Ernest Wallace and E. Adamson Hoebel, *The Comanches: Lords of the South Plains* (Norman: University of Oklahoma Press, 1952); Juan de Ulibarri, "The Diary of Juan de Ulibarri to El Cuartelejo, 1706," in Thomas, ed., *After Coronado,* p. 113. For an overview of these developments see Magnaghi, "The Indian Slave Trader," pp. 78–90.

9. Fray Alonso de Posada, "The Report of Fray Alonso de Posada in Relation to Quiviraand Teguayo," trans. S. Lyman Tyler and H. Daniel Taylor, *New Mexico Historical Review* 33 (October 1958): 301–03; Cheryl Foote, "Spanish–Indian Trade along New Mexico's Northern Frontier in the Eighteenth Century," *Journal of the West* 24 (1985): 22–33; Fray Miguel Menchero to José Villaseñor, Informe, circa 1744, Archivo General de la Nacíon, Mexico City (AGN) *Historia*, vol. 25, folio 231; "Report of . . . Serrano," in Charles W. Hackett, ed., *Historical Documents Relating to New Mexico, Nueva Vizcaya, and Approaches Thereto, to 1773* (Washington, DC: Carnegie Institution, 1937), 3: 486; Eleanor B. Adams and Fray Angélico Chávez, eds. and trans., *The Missions of New Mexico, 1776: A Description by Fray Francisco Atanasio Domínguez, with Other Contemporary Documents* (Albuquerque: University of New Mexico Press, 1956), p. 252. For a detailed study of the pre-Hispanic trade between the Plains and Pueblo Indians, see Charles L. Kenner, *A History of New Mexican–Plains Indian Relations* (Norman: University of Oklahoma Press, 1969); for a thorough study of the captive trade fairs, see Magnaghi, "The Indian Slave Trader," pp. 135–43.

10. David M. Brugge, "Some Plains Indians in the Church Records of New Mexico," *Plains Anthropologist* 10 (1965): 181–89; James H. Gunnerson and Dolores A. Gunnerson, *Ethnohistory of the High Plains* (Denver: Colorado State Office, Bureau of Land Management, 1988), pp. 49–50.

11. *Recopilación de leyes.* . . . (Madrid, 1681), libro VII, título VII, leyes III, XVII.

12. Colin M. MacLachlan and Jaime E. Rodríguez O, *The Forging of the Cosmic Race: A Reinterpretation of Colonial Mexico* (Berkeley: University of California Press, 1980),pp. 208–09, 223–28; New Mexico Genealogical Society, comp., *Albuquerque Baptisms, Archdiocese of Santa Fe, 1706–1850* (Albuquerque: New Mexico Genealogical Society, 1983), pp. 2, 4, 8, 13, 15, 17, 35, 36, 39, 51–55.

13. Adams and Chávez, *Missions of New Mexico*, p. 42.

14. "Diligencias seguidas por querella de dos Yndias Genízaras sirbientes contra sus amos," 12–15 October 1763, Spanish Archives of New Mexico (SANM), Santa Fe, microfilm reel 9, frames 524–26.

15. Pedro Alonso O'Crouley, *A Description of the Kingdom of New Spain*, trans. and ed. Sean Galvin (1774; rpt. San Francisco: John Howell Books, 1972), p. 52; Hackett, *Historical Documents*, 3: 401; Fray Joachim Rodríguez, San Ildefonso, Complaint, 14 April 1766, SANM, reel 9, frames 949–51.

16. Alfred B. Thomas, ed. and trans., *Forgotten Frontiers: A Study of the Spanish Indian Policy of Don Juan Bautista de Anza Governor of New Mexico, 1777–1787* (Norman: University of Oklahoma Press, 1932), pp. 91–92.

17. Fray Damian Martínez to Fray Juan Agustín Morfí, 1792, AGN *Historia*, vol. 25, folio 138.

18. Ibid.; Robert R. Miller, "New Mexico in the Mid-eighteenth Century: A Report Based on Governor Vélez Cachupín's Inspection," *Southwestern Historical Quarterly* 79 (October 1975): 171.

19. Frederick W. Hodge, ed., *Handbook of American Indians, North of Mexico*. Bureau of American Ethnology *Bulletin* No. 30, 2 vols. (Washington, DC: Government Printing Office, 1907–10) 1: 489.

20. Virginia Langham Olmsted, comp., *Spanish and Mexican Colonial Censuses of New Mexico, 1790, 1823, 1845* (Albuquerque: New Mexico Genealogical Society, 1975), pp. 42–44.

21. Henry W. Kelly, "Franciscan Missions of New Mexico, 1740–1760," *New Mexico Historical Review* 16 (January 1941): 68; Florence H. Ellis, "Tome and Father J.B.R.," *New Mexico Historical Review* 30 (April 1955): 93; "Declaration of Fray Miguel de Menchero, Santa Barbara, May 10, 1744," in Hackett, *Historical Documents. . .*, 3: 401–02; "Description of . . . El Paso del Río del Norte, as Given by One of Its Citizens, after Seven Years Residence There, September 1, 1773," in Hackett, *Historical Documents*, 3: 506–08; O'Crouley, *A Description*, p. 51; Oakah L. Jones, *Los Paisanos: Spanish Settlers on the Northern Frontier of New Spain* (Norman: University of Oklahoma Press, 1979), pp. 116–17; Kenner, *History of New Mexico–Plains Indian Relations*, p. 63.

22. Eleanor B. Adams, ed., *Bishop Tamarón's Visitation of New Mexico, 1760* (Albuquerque: University of New Mexico Press, 1954), p. 57; Miller, "New Mexico in the Mid-eighteenth Century," p. 176; Robert Archibald, "Cañon de Carnue: Settlement of a Grant," *New Mexico Historical Review* 51 (October 1976): 316, 319.

23. Virginia Langham Olmsted, comp., *Spanish and Mexican Censuses of New Mexico, 1750 to 1830* (Albuquerque: New Mexico Genealogical Society, 1981), pp. 1–97; John L. Kessell, *Kiva, Cross, and Crown: The Pecos Indians and New Mexico, 1540–1840* (Washington, D.C.: U.S. Department of Interior, National Park Service,1979), p. 512; Donald C. Cutter, trans., "An Anonymous Statistical Report on New Mexico in 1765," *New Mexico Historical Review* 50 (1975): 349–51; O'Crouley, *A Description*, pp. 58–59. There are few citations for genízaros in their early communities (Belén, Tomé, and Abiquiú) because they had been baptized before they arrived and were probably listed as Spanish in burial records.

24. For a definitive study on racial classification, see Magnus Mörner, *Race Mixture in the History of Latin America* (Boston: Little, Brown and Co., 1967).

25. Olmsted, *Spanish and Mexican Colonial Censuses*, p. i; Olmsted, *Censuses of New Mexico, 1790, 1823, 1845*; SANM, 1790 census, reel 12.

26. Albert H. Schroeder, "Río Grande Ethnohistory," *New Perspectives on the Pueblos* (Albuquerque: University of New Mexico Press, 1972), p. 62; Alfred B. Thomas, ed., "An Anonymous Description of New Mexico, 1818," *Southwestern Historical Quarterly* 33 (July 1929): 61.

27. Adams and Chávez, *Missions of New Mexico*, p. 42.

28. Thomas, "An Anonymous Description," p. 59; Miller, "New Mexico in the Mid-eighteenth Century," p. 178; Marc Simmons, trans., "The Chacon Economic Report of 1803," *New Mexico Historical Review* 60 (January 1985): 85; Olmsted, *Censuses of New Mexico, 1790, 1823, 1845*; SANM, 1790 census, reel 12.

29. Adams and Chávez, *Missions of New Mexico*, p. 252.

30. Josiah Gregg, *The Commerce of the Prairies*, ed. Milo Milton Quaife (New York: The Citadel Press, 1968), p. 219.

31. Kessell, *Kiva, Cross and Crown*, p. 512; Miller, "New Mexico in the Mid-eighteenth Century," p. 176.

32. "Declaration of . . . Menchero . . . 1744," Hackett, *Historical Documents*, 3: 402; Oakah L. Jones, *Pueblo Warriors and Spanish Conquest* (Norman: University of Oklahoma Press, 1966), p. 175.

33. Report of Caballero de Croix, Mexico, 2 July 1777, SANM, reel 10, frame 925; [Chacon] "Extracto de las novedades occuridas en la Provincia del Nuevo Mexico desde 4 de octubre haron 29 de noviembre . . . 1800," Santa Fe, 24 November 1800, SANM, reel 14 frame 652. Santa Fe, 24 November 1800, SANM, reel 14, frame 652; Joseph Manuel de Ochoa, Ojo de Anaya, 30 November 1800, SANM, reel 14, frames 658–59; Comandante General Salcedo to Governor Maynez, Chihuahua, 12 August 1808; Governor Maynez/Manrrique to Comandante General Salcedo, Santa Fe, 20 June 1809, SANM, reel 16, frames 596, 907–09.

34. Adams and Chávez, *Missions of New Mexico*, p. 113.

35. [Chacon to Pedro de Nava], Santa Fe, 10 June 1800, SANM, reel 14, frames 548–49.

36. David J. Weber, *The Mexican Frontier, 1821–1846: The American Southwest under Mexico* (Albuquerque: University of New Mexico Press, 1982), p. 213; trial of *genízaros* for sedition, Santa Fe–Chihuahua, 9 December 1807 to 28 March 1808, SANM, reel 15, frames 1099–1117.

37. Olmsted, *Censuses of New Mexico, 1790, 1823, 1845*; SANM, 1790 census, reel 12; Ralph E. Twitchell, *The Spanish Archives of New Mexico*, 2 vols. (Cedar Rapids, IA: The Torch Press, 1914), 1: 1138.

38. Kenner, *A History of New Mexico–Plains Indian Relations*, p. 64; Jones, *Los Paisanos*, p. 149. For studies of penitentes, see Marta Weigle, *Brothers of Light, Brothers of Blood: The Penitentes of the Southwest* (Albuquerque: University of New Mexico Press, 1976); Lorayne Horka-Follick, *Los Hermanos Penitentes: A Vestige of Medievalism in Southwestern United States* (Los Angeles: Westernlore Press, 1969); and Fray Angélico Chávez, "The Penitentes of New Mexico," *New Mexico Historical Review* 29 (April 1954): 97–123.

39. Adams and Chávez, *Missions of New Mexico*, pp. 126, 259, 336.

40. Thomas James, *Three Years among the Indians and Mexicans* (Lincoln: University of Nebraska Press, 1984), pp. 58, 68, 71, 80, 108; Gregg, *Commerce of the Prairies*, p. 142.

41. Kenner, *A History of New Mexican–Plains Indian Relations*, p. 63.

42. Kenner, *A History of New Mexican–Plains Indian Relations*, pp. 63, 79; James, *Three Years*, pp. 108, 110; Gregg, *Commerce of the Prairies*, p. 157.

43. The controversy over Gonzáles's origins is best traced in Janet Lecompte, *Rebellion in Río Arriba, 1837* (Albuquerque: University of New Mexico Press, 1985), pp. 36–75. Fray Angelico Chavez, "José Gonzáles, Genízaro Governor," *New Mexico Historical Review* 30 (1955): 190–94, takes the position that Gonzáles was a genízaro, stating that Gonzáles escaped after the battle of Pojoaque and died several months later.

44. Schroeder, "Río Grande Ethnohistory," p. 62.

†

8
Epilogue
Ralph H. Vigil

The stark division between the Spaniards of antiquity and modern persons of Mexican, Mexican American, Chicano, and Hispanic heritage has been one of the most striking aspects of Anglo-Hispano relations since 1848. After that date, the unified heritage of the colonial period fractured, exalting dead Spaniards and despising living Mexicans. The polarized Hispanic heritage, a product of selective interpretation arising from political and cultural conflict in the nineteenth century, has also influenced the Chicano's search for a new identity.

Because the differences between Spaniards, Mexicans, New Mexicans, and other Hispanics before 1850 were "regional distinctions occurring within a similar culture," the absurd dichotomy between what is Spanish and what is Mexican has been accurately described as schizophrenic. "Regular" Americans and Spanish-speaking borderlanders, however, accepted and cultivated this pernicious mythology and came to see "the Spanish-speaking as living at once in two disharmonious worlds, one mythic, and the other real. The mythic world emphasizes the 'Spanish' past — carefree, unchanging, and enveloped in a religious aura; the other is a 'Mexican' world — disagreeable, mundane, potentially violent."[1]

Individuals such as Walter Prescott Webb have stressed race and ignored culture, making the historical experience of Spanish-speaking borderlanders of New Mexico, Texas, and California in late colonial times less European and more Indian. Such an approach ignores historical reality, for the Spaniards who came to the New World were not an ethnically homogeneous people. Genetically and culturally, the aboriginal tribes of Spain absorbed a long series of invaders, colonizers, and medieval slaves, including Slavs and Africans. Moslems and

Jews also had a great cultural influence on the peninsula. All of these elements became part of the Spanish population and did not change the somatic composition of the majority of Iberians. The Spanish were described in the early sixteenth century as dark-skinned, short, haughty people inclined to war, dissimulation, and the eating of Guinea pepper with their food.[2] In short, Spaniards had experienced ethnic and racial miscegenation *before* their arrival in America. Racial and cultural *mestizaje* continued in the New World and has become "the most interesting, significant and enduring contribution of Latin America to a world poisoned by deeply rooted racism."[3]

The idea that Hispanics are a mixture of Africa and America and that even Spain had "ceased to be European because of her African blood" is at least as old as the nationalistic and romantic historiography of Spanish American revolutionaries such as Simón Bolívar.[4] The image of the Hispanic people — variously called Latins, Latin Americans, Latinos, Mexicans, Mexican Americans, Spanish Americans, Spanish-surname, Spanish-speaking, Chicano, or Hispano — as genetically or culturally "un-European" was fully developed in the last half of the nineteenth century, a period marked by obsessive racialism, intolerance, nationalism, and colonial imperialism. More recently, ideas of race and racialism have been subsumed, at least in part, by ideas of "ethnicity," and "racial traits" usually are called "cultural traits" or "national character." But whatever terms one uses, the conviction that ethnic groups are more different than alike in thought and action remains with us. In fact, present-day literature about American minorities all too often takes for granted the desirability of assimilation, and a great number of U.S. citizens know little about Hispanics, Mexicans, Mexican Americans, Chicanos, or themselves.

Most non-Hispanics, as well as a good number of Hispanics, continue to make facile distinctions between Hispanics north and south of the border. In addition to perpetuating caricatures such as the "Latin lover," the "Frito Bandito," and the apelike villain found in the motion picture based on B. Traven's *The Treasure of the Sierra Madre*, non-Hispanic Americans tend to describe Mexicans and other Latinos as a dark-skinned, quick-tempered, emotional people.[5] Other generalizations and stereotypes about Mexicans have been around since at least 1836. Pejorative adjectives such as "cruel," "lazy," "backward," and "simple" have been frequently used to describe Mexicans, and slurs such as "greaser" and "spic" are part of the American vocabulary.

The problem of understanding Hispanics, a term used by government and media, is further complicated by their heterogeneity. Historically and culturally, Hispanics are as diverse as any group of people. Mexican Americans, for example, are individually either new immigrants, descendants of immigrants who arrived in the first quarter of the twentieth century, or members of a "conquered minority" who trace their ancestry back to the Spanish and Mexican pioneers who established the viceroyalty of New Spain and the kingdom of New Mexico.

Hispanics in the United States before 1960 numbered 3.1 million and included people born in Mexico, Central and South America, the Antilles, and Spain. Because the 1970 census broadened the definition by including "the racial origin of respondents, no matter the accident of birthplace," 9.1 million Hispanics were counted that year. The Census Bureau calculated that there were 12 million Hispanic Americans in 1978 but noted that if the estimated 7.4 million illegal aliens were added to this figure, Hispanics numbered more than 19 million, or about 9 percent of the total population.[6]

The rapid population growth of Hispanics in the United States is attributable to its largest single group, called by one study "the Mexican origin population."[7] This group grew from 4.5 million in 1970 to 8.7 million in 1980, a 93 percent gain in size. Although 83 percent of the Mexican American population lived in the Southwest in the 1980s, the states of Florida, Illinois, Ohio, and Washington each had more than 50,000 people of Mexican origin. Other Mexican Americans had moved to the Great Plains and Midwest, "attracted by better-paying jobs and the region's homespun values."[8] A newspaper article describing this "invasion" into America's heartland stated that although the Hispanic population of the region was "small and most Midwest states remain overwhelmingly white, the percentage increases are significant."[9] As this quotation illustrates, Mexican Americans are viewed as nonwhite migrants attracted to the Great Plains and upper Midwest "because of its progressive traditions and liberal social programs."[10] Mexican Americans remain in the eyes of heartlanders a marginal ethnic or racial group. "The newcomers include former big-city residents, migrants desperate to escape backbreaking lives, immigrants legalized in the 1986 amnesty program, and the down-and-out from the border."[11]

This classification of Mexican Americans poses a problem for Hispanics. One definition of identity is "something that is assigned by persons to other persons" — in this case, something assigned by super-ordinate whites to a subordinate "nonwhite" group called Hispanics. Thus, the question "Who am I?" immediately poses another question for the individual and the group: "Who am I in the eyes of others?"[12] In order to more fully understand this question of image and how it has affected the Hispanic present, one has to examine the beliefs that have influenced relationships between Mexican Americans and "unhyphenated" Americans.

When Anglo-Americans (a catch-all expression) formally assumed control of the Southwest in 1848, they were accustomed to regarding Hispanics as an inferior people. The English and Spaniards were products of different, mutually hostile Europes, and anti-Spanish views were used by the English to justify international rivalry in both Old World and New in the seventeenth and eighteenth centuries. Spaniards were stereotyped by northern Europeans as cruel, intolerant, fanatically superstitious, imperialistic, greedy, hypocritical, immoral, decadent, and plundering. In contrast, English people were portrayed as liberty-loving, industrious homemakers and state builders.[13]

In addition to their Hispanophobia, the English and Anglo-Americans had well-formed ideas about the character of Indians and Africans at the time they met the Mexicans. Hence, they immediately compared these newly conquered people to those whom they had persecuted in the process of establishing the United States.[14] Anglo-Americans initially possessed no single image of Native Americans, but on the frontier Indians were usually viewed by military officers and settlers as ignoble savages, the counterimage of all that was "good, decent, Christian, and American." By the early nineteenth century, Anglo-American backwoods settlers regarded "the Indian with a degree of terror and hatred, similar to that which he feels towards the rattlesnake or panther, and which can neither be removed by argument, nor appeased by anything but the destruction of its object."[15]

The image of blacks in the Anglo-American psyche has been discussed by many writers, but the best treatment was offered by Winthrop Jordan.[16] Britishers were culturally disposed to see evil and ugliness in darker-skinned Africans, Jordan argued, and racial prejudice and labor needs soon brought about the mass enslavement and importation of Africans into the English colonies. After the colonies gained their independence, Africans were socially and legally defined as less than human, and slavery became a "divine trust" in Southern minds.[17]

Images of the Mexican in American literature have been thoroughly studied by Cecil Robinson.[18] His interpretations confirm Leslie Fiedler's contention that darker peoples, including Spaniards, represent anticivilization (the wilderness) and the impulsive life (the id) to those in the paleface majority.[19] Anglo-Americans quickly condemned Mexican Catholicism and stated that Mexicans were morbidly preoccupied with death, prone to violent crimes and theft, indifferent to cleanliness, and innately lazy and corrupt. Perhaps even more important than these alleged defects was Anglo-Americans' horror of racial mixture. Anglos felt that because Spaniards had "lowered themselves to a state of general cohabitation with the Indians," they had lost the right to be considered members of the "white" race.[20] Francis Parkman described Spaniards as "dark" and "slavish looking" people who gazed "stupidly out from beneath their broad hats." Mexicans were "swarthy, ignoble" people with "brutish faces." They were also squalid and lower than Indians in order of merit. One could not concede to them the honorable title of "whites";[21] quite the opposite — Mexicans were occasionally compared to Negroes. An Anglo-Texan near the Brazos River told Frederick Law Olmsted in the 1850s that Mexico's people were bigoted and ignorant, "as black as niggers any way, and ten times as treacherous."[22] Anglos in the 1840s considered Santa Fe "a dirty and inferior place" whose inhabitants were "mainly occupied in gambling, drunken fandangoes and debaucheries."[23]

As the nineteenth century ran its course, Mexican stereotypes became more complex. John Russell Bartlett, for example, claimed that a vast gulf intervened between, on the one hand, "a few respectable old Spanish families at El Paso, who possess much intelligence, as well as that elegance and dignity of manner which characterized their ancestors," and, on the other hand, the masses, who were "a mixed breed, possessing none of the virtue of their European ancestors, but all their vices, with those of the aborigines superadded."[24] The ambivalent Josiah Gregg observed that there were no Africans, mulattoes, nor *zambos* in New Mexico, but he did assert that of the 60,000 or more souls estimated as white or Spanish in 1841, 1,000 were white Creoles and the remainder were mestizos.[25]

Lewis H. Garrard thought Charles Bent's wife, María Ignacia Jaramillo, a handsome woman and her sister a beauty, but he was still of the opinion that Mexican women had "a depraved moral education" and that their attraction was of the "baser sort."[26] More recently, David Lavender in *Bent's Fort* told his readers that Charles Bent's wife had "a lighter complexion than most Mexican women boasted."[27] Even Carey McWilliams asserted that New Mexicans were divided into two major classes, the rich and the poor: "To some extent, the division marked a caste as well as a class differentiation, for the *ricos* were 'lighter,' more 'Spanish,' than the *pobres.*"[28]

The Spanish-speaking people of the southern Plains and the greater Southwest clearly were a victimized out-group by 1900, a fact largely explained by the influx of new people and a new economic order that replaced the older agrarian economy in the region. But despite the conflict between Anglos and Hispanics, the descendants of the more than 80,000 Mexicans who became subjects of this nation in its triumphant march to the Pacific would have been assimilated and become "regular Americans" if they had remained a small ethnic group. However, their numbers became too great. Mexican immigration began as early as 1849, after gold was discovered in California, and by 1930 there were perhaps 1.2 million persons of Mexican descent in the Southwest. A study by Richard L. Nostrand noted that in 1970 about 6.2 million people of Mexican ancestry resided in the region, and "an additional contingent, nearly 3,100,000 in size, had found its way to the non-southwestern states."[29]

In his study of the Spanish-speaking Californians, Leonard Pitt noted that ethnic groups in the United States are destined "to be thrown together with people of 'their own kind' whom they neither know nor particularly like — perhaps even despise."[30] Both in the nineteenth and twentieth centuries, wherever Mexican immigrants have located in large numbers, all of the Spanish-surnamed people ("Hispanics") have been lumped together by non-Hispanics ("Anglos"). Given the diversity to be found in both groups, the terms "Hispanic" and "Anglo" are essentially meaningless, except in terms of the real or imagined differences between the two groups.

At the beginning of the century, Mexican Americans were "Spaniards" if they had social and economic power and "Mexicans" if they were poor. Then came the great migration. Mexicans lacking opportunity south of the border crossed the Río Grande in response to the demand for unskilled labor by large-scale fruit and vegetable growers (especially sugar beet companies), railroad companies, ranchers, contractors, and the like. Mexican laborers were initially concentrated along the border, but by 1930 settlements of Mexicans imported by the rail lines were found in Kansas and Nebraska. Other Mexicans worked in the steel mills, stockyards, tanneries, and packing plants of the Midwest, and the Mexican colony of Detroit had a population of 15,000 in 1928.

Across the nation, non-Hispanics, whether of "pure American stock" or of more recent vintage, have lumped the Spanish-speaking together as "aliens," a racially and culturally distinct non-Western people. It has also been claimed that Mexican immigrants, whether permanent or temporary, legal or illegal, have created below-minimum wage labor pools. Indeed, the negative stereotype attributed to Hispanics is largely due to the nature of their employment. However, this is not entirely the fault of the immigrants. Consider the *bracero* program, which ended in 1964 but arose as a war measure in 1942. By this agreement with Mexico, the U.S. government subsidized American growers by allowing the importation of low-wage workers for temporary jobs in agriculture.[31] The program benefited farmers, because the U.S. government acted as their labor contractor, but it also prevented the unionization of Mexican American farm workers.

The end of the bracero program allowed organizers such as César Chávez to improve the lot of farm workers, but Mexican Americans today are still underrepresented in professional, technical, and managerial jobs. Moreover, it appears that the employment and occupational patterns of Mexican Americans are institutionalized to serve the needs of a secondary labor market. This labor market, characterized by dead-end jobs, "was created and is maintained by established elements of American society and is actually being extended and perpetuated by current agency efforts to train minority workers."[32] Hispanic family income in 1990 was "further below the income of the typical white family than at any other time." The main reason for this gap was the restructuring of the economy in the last decade, one effect being the acceleration of "an economic ghettoizing of Hispanics into low-paying service sector employment."[33] The trend will probably continue, given the problems of inadequate Hispanic education and their present occupational profile.

The Borderlands: "Dawn of American History"

It is obvious that the Hispanics annexed by conquest in 1848 were here first. Moreover, because our nation's European heritage begins in the Hispanic borderlands, and because the cultural roots of millions of Americans are found there, borderlands research is not only "a study of the dawn and development of American history." Rather, the region's history "provides a measuring scale on which the elements of cultural borrowing, ethnic assimilation, and the inter-racial tensions inevitable in these processes, can be assayed."[34]

Present-day Americans whose ancestors settled the borderlands identify with a land first inhabited by Mexican Spaniards (*españoles mexicanos*) as early as 1598. But how does one deal with what Arthur M. Corwin calls the biggest non sequitur of all, borrowed from Carey McWilliams' *North from Mexico*: "namely, that the historical heritage of the massive La Raza or Chicano migration that flowed in from twentieth-century Mexico is somehow the direct lineal descendant of the historical experience of Hispanos, Tejanos, and Californios settled in small, isolated enclaves on the distant rim of the Spanish empire"?[35]

The answer to the above question depends on whether one stresses nationalism or culture. It is true that Mexican immigrants who arrived after the turn of the century demonstrated an exuberant loyalty to the country they had left, waxed nostalgic for "beloved Mexico" in their songs, and celebrated Cinco de Mayo and El Grito de Dolores. However, these expressions of "puro mexicano" arose from the same "sense of cleavage or opposition to the Anglos" found among those Hispanos who "were already very much a part of the landscape when the Anglo-Americans came to the Southwest."[36] The Hispanos felt themselves to be foreigners in their native land and looked back to a Spanish past for their roots; the Mexicans felt themselves to be foreigners in Anglo America and looked to Mexico for a sense of identity. As McWilliams correctly noted, regardless of the differences apparent among Hispanics concerning nomenclature, historical identity, or ideology, the dichotomy between the terms "Anglo" and "Hispano," "*gabacho*" and "Mexican," or "*gringo*" and "Latino" gives cohesion to the group.[37]

Moreover, Hispanos call themselves *mexicanos*. Although this term has a purely cultural or geographic connotation, indicating affiliation with New Mexico rather than with Old Mexico or the present-day Mexican republic, the word "mexicano" is also used in reference to language, music, and traditional foods. As one Spanish anthropologist has noted, "the last two elements are truly Mexican and we may also consider the language as an extension or type of the Spanish of Mexico."[38]

Not only do Hispanos call themselves "mexicanos," they also call themselves members of *la raza* — literally, "the race." These terms, however, should *not* be taken literally; they refer not to nationality or race but rather to "a concept of culture" that cannot be conveyed by English equivalents or other Spanish terms.[39] The word "mexicano" in the narrowest sense refers to a regional subculture of the Upper Río Grande Basin, but in a wider sense it links native New Mexicans to a past in which their land was a colony of Spain and later a part of Mexico. By rejecting the term "Mexican" in the twentieth century, native New Mexicans distinguished themselves from Mexican immigrants (*surumatos*), and by adopting the self-referent "Spanish American" they asserted their Iberian heritage, still evident in their language, given names, and folklore. The term "la raza" is frequently used by older Hispanos to refer to their peoplehood, rooted in a shared history and a culture in which the family is considered more important than the individual.

The Search for Identity

Hispanos of New Mexico and southern Colorado remain a culturally distinct group. Though they now speak "Mexican Spanish," they borrow expressions and cultural references from English. As for commerce, education, entertainment, news, and politics, they live in an Anglo-oriented environment. This blending of Mexican and Anglo-American influences has occurred among a people living in their traditional land and maintaining "traditional values." What blending, then, has been experienced by Hispanos and Mexican immigrants who have moved to small towns in the central and northern Great Plains? What of those living in Omaha, Oklahoma City, Kansas City, Topeka, and other large urban centers?

The *americanos* who settled in the Hispano homeland after 1850 gave the natives words, phrases, and idiomatic expressions, which the natives Hispanicized. More recently, the workplace, the automobile, schools, and the mass media have acted "as instruments of information and entertainment, and as agents of manipulation and indoctrination,"[40] making for a common way of life and the modification of values, attitudes, and habits. Acculturation and its contradictions have made for cultural conflict and increased the desire for social and economic change. The attempt to create a sense of identity for Hispan-

ics in New Mexico arose primarily among younger Chicanos and accul-
turated activists. In fact, the principal leader of the Chicano
movement in New Mexico of the 1960s was the Texas-born Reies
López Tijerina, an Assembly-of-God Bible Institute student, cross-
country evangelist, and utopian colonizer-turned-reformer.[41]

Borrowings from English were accompanied by words and expressions brought by braceros at the turn of the century. By 1910 "Mexican
Spanish" had begun to influence the Spanish spoken by New Mexicans. It was also at this time that Mexican nationals who took up residence in the Southwest gave a literary impetus to Mexican language
and culture. Through clubs, libraries, and publications, these people
served immigrants who spoke no English and benefited bilingual
Americans of Spanish descent, called "manitos" by the migrants.[42]
Because language is culture's morphology and because Hispanos today
live in an Anglo-oriented environment "where all facets of daily living
(commerce, education, entertainment, local and national news com-
munications, politics, etc.) use English for their expression,"[43] they
have shifted to English. It is also evident that the folk culture of Hispanos has changed: They have been shaped by the dominant culture
into consumers of products, news, and entertainment.

If cultural change has been rapid in the Hispano homeland, where
the archaic local dialect is inevitably giving way to English and Mexican Spanish,[44] what has been the effect of the Great Plains environment on Hispanics from the Southwest or Mexico? Hispanics on the
Great Plains, isolated from communities they once called home, have
adapted to American culture and the customs of other ethnic groups
living in the region. But because of their occupational patterns and
the traditional hostility of old-stock Americans, Mexicans and Hispanos have been perceived as a nonwhite immigrant group occupying an
intermediate position in a social order that places persons from the
British Isles at the top and African Americans at the bottom.

One study of seventeen ethnic groups in Nebraska concluded that
persons who traced their national origins to Mexico and Africa were
the least assimilated. For these two ethnic groups, minority status has
been an important cause of their high social distance from the dominant population and their low socioeconomic status.[45] In short, discrimination against Hispanics and African Americans has probably
enhanced "psychological identification" with origins and predisposed
both groups to believe that they are culturally different and victims of
economic and educational oppression.

Mexican Americans, the largest Hispanic ethnic group living in the Great Plains, initially struggled for equal rights. Although there has been no definitive study of Mexican and Mexican American attempts to end police brutality, economic discrimination, and negative features of life in Mexican communities that have been portrayed in the press, it is clear that the struggle for civil rights has been the principal factor in the gradual creation of ethnic identity. Hispanic political activity placed little if any stress on culture until the 1960s,when the Chicano movement began constructing a new, positive image for Mexican Americans in the United States. This ideology, which arose in the Southwest, has led to the development of ethnic studies and ethnic literature and drama, leading to a new conception of the Mexican American past and present.

Because Chicano studies were originally focused on an intense but simplistic concern with defining Chicano ethnic identity, Hispanic culture was not placed in historical perspective. The new image projected by Chicanos was a healthy antidote to the myth of the Mexican American past and contemporary negative images created by "regular Americans"; however, some activists went to extremes, rejecting older terms such as "Spanish American" and "Mexican American," asserting that the Southwest was the original home of the ancient Aztecs, even proclaiming the independence of a mestizo nation. "Brown power" was identified as cultural nationalism, and Chicanos were described as the descendants of Aztlán, the sometime homeland of the Aztecs prior to their migration south in approximately 1168.[46] Chicano ideology tended to emphasize Indian heritage, romanticized by subjective interpretation, and to exalt "Indian" and "mestizo" heroes; therefore, the Hispanic heritage remained polarized. New myths arose in which the Chicano — a trilingual, bronze descendent of Mexican Indians and African slaves in some versions — "emerges in an all too angelic light, depicted in verbal hues unrecognizable to students of human nature."[47]

Chicano activists, in dismissing the Spanish past, obviously failed to acknowledge the cultural influence of Spain in America, most apparent in the language and religion of Mexican migrants to the United States. They also overlooked generational change and the "Americanizing" of the migrants' descendants, who created "an eclectic ideology that at times has drawn inspiration from the Black experience, the Latin American revolutionary experience, and the Mexican revolutionary tradition."[48] Another weakness of *chicanismo* was its failure to recognize the strong relationship between economics and values and how identity has been influenced by the minority experience.

One study of three southwestern cities has shown that the Mexican American poor are more "traditional" than those with higher incomes. Another study of Mexican American, black, and Anglo-American migrants of Racine, Wisconsin, found that blacks and Mexican Americans "had a very similar world view, and it is dramatically different from the world view of Anglo-Americans. This is true even when income is controlled. It suggests that the minority experience may be at least as significant in affecting values as is the particular cultural heritage."[49] Both of these studies suggest that the reputed or real differences between Mexican Americans and other Americans are determined as much by social class, education, and related socioeconomic conditions as they are by alleged cultural values.

In her discussion of Mexican American language and culture, Joan Moore observed that "Anglos and Mexicans (and a certain amount of the scholarly literature) continue to perpetuate clearly formulated but often inconsistent and weakly substantiated ideas about Mexican American culture."[50] Most of the literature that attempts to define Mexican "character" or identity refers to the mestizo heritage of this ethnic group and focuses "on the traits of the most downtrodden members of the society as the symbol for the whole nation."[51] In reality, this ethnic group is extremely heterogeneous. On some issues the social distance between generations of Mexican Americans is greater than the social distance between "Mexicans" and "Anglos," and this generational shift, the rising number of out-group marriages, and increased contact with Anglo-Americans and other Hispanic groups has changed perceptions. Moore has noted that Mexican Americans "have no very clear consensus on whether they are a racial group, a cultural group, or even if they are white or nonwhite." They do, however, have "a vague sense of ethnic identity, a compelling feeling of belonging — but to *what* is left relatively unconceptualized."[52]

This vague sense of identity, this "what" and its difference from the larger society, persists — whether based on tradition or contemporary reality, whether considered distinct or syncretic, self-shaped or imposed, or a mixture of the view from without and within. In much the same way that Chicano ideology has identified culture with political activism — what one may call the struggle of an internally colonized people against racism, exploitation, and genocide in the

Southwest — a cultural-political Latino identity has arisen among Mexican Americans (Chicanos) and Puerto Ricans (Boricuas) in Chicago.[53] Created by community organization leaders of the Hispanic community and based upon presumed cultural characteristics and marginality, this type of situational group consciousness becomes operative when the Spanish-speaking address citywide issues of concern and interest to both groups.

Although *latinismo* in Chicago is "situationally specific" rather than "historically fixed" or an "inherited type of group form and identity," it may be viewed as an identity based upon shared historical experiences and "an awareness of being different from other social groups in the United States."[54] In short, it appears that Mexican Americans, Puerto Ricans, Cubans, and Central and South Americans have developed an awareness of their shared Hispanic tradition. The effort to resist discrimination and exploitation collectively and promote their interests has created, in the words of one Puerto Rican community leader, "a great deal of commonality and experience in these groups. This may very well bring us back to Spain."[55]

This return to Spain, a return to history, places the Hispanic cultural heritage within its proper frame of reference. This is not to say that Hispanics have not changed over the centuries, nor does a historical explanation sufficiently explain Hispanics or any other people. History does, however, demonstrate that Hispanics in the Americas have a cultural tie with the Iberian peninsula. Moreover, the history of Latin American colonization confirms that this polarized heritage was unified until the nineteenth century. As history has become more specialized, historians have tended to compartmentalize the Hispanic heritage chronologically, geographically, and nationally. Those following Herbert Eugene Bolton's lead have published an enormous quantity of material on the Spanish borderlands. More recently, an admirable synthesis of the Mexican frontier before it became the U.S. Southwest has shed more light on this period.[56] By the 1960s, Mexican Americans were no longer forgotten; they and other Hispanic groups had become part of the new history being taught in the schools.

The Spanish Legacy

In 1992, the quincentennial of Columbus's first voyage to the New World, there was much focus on Hispanic heritage's peculiar and contested legacy. In some instances, little if any unity between the various Hispanic groups was seen because the history of Hispanics has been assigned geographical, chronological, racial, and cultural boundaries. The implication of such compartmentalization is that the fields of Spanish, Latin American, Mexican, borderlands, and Western history are so distinct one from the other that there is more difference than unity to the Hispanic heritage. Another hotly contested issue was the contention that in contrast to the English, who settled America, the few Spaniards that crossed the Atlantic merely exploited Native Americans. Hence, for those Hispanics who identify with the indigenous past, "Latin America was created by a crime of genocide initiated by Columbus and directed against Native Americans."[57]

The idea that Hispanics in general are a non-Western people who have little cultural affinity with Spain is not new. Since Mexican independence and increasingly after the 1910 Mexican Revolution, there has been an ongoing debate between the *hispanista* and *indigenista* schools of interpretation concerning the Mexican past. The defenders of Spain, such as Lucas Alamán, considered native societies less advanced than Spanish society and viewed the conquest and Europeanization as positive developments. By contrast, indigenistas imply or openly state "that the native societies and cultures were equal, even superior," to the European and mixed ones that displaced them. They thus regard the Spanish conquest and colonization as "an unfortunate interruption in a native New World cultural evolution that might have produced further but now unknowable wonders."[58]

To define the Hispanic heritage geographically, chronologically, or in terms of bloodlines ("as though we were dealing with race horses")[59] misses an essential point that Herbert Eugene Bolton and various of his successors have stressed. Hispanic history, whether at the local, regional, or national level, is not an isolated history. "It is a concept, a way of life, a cultural expression" of a Spanish frontier that is part of a "greater America" settled and transformed by various European nations.[60] In this sense, Hispanic history is the history of frontiers in which various cultures have met, clashed, and blended. Given this perspective, Southwestern history of the United States and the history of the Great Plains is a part of European, Indian, Mexican, and U.S. history that cannot be fully understood except in the context of the epic of greater America. Not only does it include local, state, regional, national, and international history, it is also one example of "phases common to most portions of the entire Western Hemisphere."[61]

Given this wider vision, the regional history of the United States from the Upper Missouri to the Far West embraces the pre-Columbian civilizations, European exploration and colonization, racial mixture, cultural fusion, international rivalry, the rise of independent nations following the American revolutions, and the planting of Anglo-American political institutions and culture in the former Spanish-Mexican borderlands. It also encompasses the present efforts of Hispanics and Indians to find their place in the sun of a region that was first traveled and claimed by Spaniards who, for good or ill, established a historical and cultural legacy that became truly American both in its local and hemispheric sense.

Though Anglo-Americans and Hispanic Americans are both products of Western civilizations, they are children of different European nations (one Protestant and the other Catholic) and rivals for empire. Their imperial systems had similar features, but the distinguishing feature of the empire of Charles V was its universalist claims. The Spanish kings linked the discovery of America "to the millenarian and apocalyptic vision of converting all the races of the world. This seemed to be the Spanish mission, and therefore the Spaniards were the chosen people, their king the 'emperor saviour.' "[62] Rather than being described as a crusade for Christianity, however, the Spanish conquest is frequently painted in the darkest colors. Moreover, an abundant body of evidence suggests that the Black Legend's content is horribly true. Military conquest in the New World was accompanied, or shortly followed, by settlement, appropriation of Indian lands, and the exploitation of the natives by labor systems and practices that contributed to the disastrous demographic decline of the Indian populations. Further, Indians under Spanish rule became a deculturated minority group victimized by prejudice and discrimination, and Spanish laws written for their protection were often ignored.

Granted the Black Legend's essential truth, it still has to be definitely proved that ancient Mexico, for example, was a New World Eden, as some indigenistas have claimed. Nor is it fair for U.S. historians to decry the Spanish conquest and compare Columbus and the Catholic kings with contemporary totalitarians while neglecting to mention that "we are living in a land wrested from the Indians in a conquest just as ruthless and infinitely more thorough than that of Mexico."[63] Moreover, although all conquests are evil, it may also be argued that the Spanish imperial enterprise had positive features lacking in other conquests. Spain joined military power to militant spiritual action, and although the desire to win converts for the faith may have gone hand-in-hand with the desire for earthly glory and riches, many authorities have agreed that "no other nation made so continuous or so passionate an attempt to discover what was the just treatment for the native peoples under its jurisdiction than Spaniards."[64]

Not all Spaniards exploited Indians, and a significant number were members of a pro-Indian party that championed the rights of the native population. The greatest of these reformers was Bartolomé de Las Casas.[65] Crown officials and friars who opposed the evils of the conquest were themselves Spaniards, representatives "of an important aspect of Spanish character, an aspect that is Christian, compassionate, egalitarian, and unimpeachable. In this view, a Spain that could produce a figure such as Las Casas cannot be condemned out of hand as morally irresponsible."[66] By contrast, the English imperial enterprise is marked by values that a "less enlightened" age denounced as social vices; this enterprise lacked spokesmen such as Las Casas or nineteenth-century New Mexico's Father Antonio José Martínez.[67] Most of the English did not view Indians as lost sheep to be brought into the fold or as a necessary part of society, and "counterparts to the friars and the padre rarely figured in the story of the Anglo-American westward movement,"[68] Roger Williams and a few other clergymen excepted.

Great as were the faults of Spain in the New World, Castile transmitted its culture and institutions to the American colonies. Colonial society in Spanish America reflected the good intentions of the crown and church as well as the spirit of exploitation characteristic of all frontier societies. The strata of the hierarchic society resembled the feudal system of the Middle Ages, but vertical social mobility was possible, and genetic and cultural mixture was common. Intermarriage with the Indian population was permitted and encouraged by government and religious leaders as early as 1501. By the end of the eighteenth century, the miscegenation begun by Hernán Cortés and his fellow adventurers was so complete that few individuals of "pure" race, whether Indian or Spaniard, were to be found in Mexico. Individuals were enrolled into the social order on the basis of wealth rather than racial purity. Moreover, through interracial concubinage and marriage with Africans, mulatto descendants of the conquerors were "innumerable" by the early seventeenth century.[69] Although the trace of black ancestry was considered a mark of vicious origin, it was possible for wealthy mulattoes in the eighteenth century to purchase documents establishing their legal whiteness. In fact, the legal integration of Africans at the time of independence, when slavery was abolished, "was but the confirmation of a socially sanctioned situation, which was the inevitable result of the contradiction of the colonial system."[70]

Mexico's far northern frontier was especially characterized by miscegenation. Indeed, New Mexico is the best example in the U.S. Southwest of a genetically mestizo but culturally and institutionally Spanish region. A considerable number of Hispanicized and Christianized Indians (*genízaros*) were to be found in the towns of Abiquiú, Belén, and Tomé in the late eighteenth century. They received Spanish surnames, learned the Spanish language, married into the surrounding Spanish families, and in time became part of the ascribed Spanish population. There were in 1799 approximately 10,369 Indians and 23,769 Spaniards in New Mexico, if by Spaniards we designate those who followed Spanish sociocultural patterns in a society removed from an exaggerated racist conception and flexible to an extreme.[71] Don Pedro Pino, New Mexico's representative in the Cádiz assembly that produced the Spanish Constitution of 1812, reported to his fellow deputies that there were only two types of people in his province: Spaniards and Indians. There were no castes of people of African origin, and the Pueblo Indians hardly differed from the Spaniards.[72]

California, settled at a later date than New Mexico, also had a rich Hispanic tradition. As late as 1826 isolation made for an essentially medieval and clerical society, and the "Spanish heritage was still in strong evidence." Following Mexican independence, the elevation of the rancheros, and the secularization of the missions, the old value system continued. The gentry regarded themselves as grandees without a court, as aristocrats in a republic, and "the rancheros, who had behaved like aristocrats even while poor, eased into affluence naturally, as if living up to a pre-established level of life — say, that of Spain in the eighteenth century."[73] Among the gentry of Mexican California was Pio Pico, governor and grandson of a mestizo grandfather and a mulatto grandmother; their children served as soldiers, acquired property, and rose in social status.[74]

Because Spain was in the Mississippi Valley, officially, for less than thirty-eight years (1762–1800) and there were very few Spaniards in Louisiana, the colonial administration used former French subjects in its efforts to control the Indian nations of the Upper Missouri through trade, presents, and symbols of chiefly authority.

Results were mixed. In the lower Mississippi Valley the Spanish used Scottish traders to maintain the friendship and support of the southern Indians.[75] Following Pinckney's Treaty (1795) and Spain's agreement to move all garrisons from land north of the 31st parallel, the chief of Spain's Chickasaw allies lamented that now that the Spanish king had abandoned them, they would lose their lands to the Americans, "who have no other desire than to fall upon us and take our country, who perhaps wish to kill us as though we were bears in order to seize our lands more quickly."[76]

The opinions expressed by the Chickasaw chief are supported by the Declaration of Independence and the U.S. Constitution. The first document described Native Americans as "merciless Indian Savages, whose known rule of warfare, is an indistinguishable destruction of all ages, sexes, and conditions." The second document apportioned representation in the lower house by the three-fifths compromise and excluded "Indians not taxed." One may also note that in English and Anglo America, there was no equivalent of the "mulatto escape hatch" to be found in Spanish American society. As Charles E. O'Neill has noted: "In this era of black studies one awaits fuller treatment of the black Louisianan who could be a militiaman in 1790 — but not fifty or a hundred years later."[77]

Rather than conducting a policy of "ethnocide," Spain in America created a multiethnic society that had positive features lacking in other colonization efforts. As Jacques Lafaye and James Lockhart state, "One need only compare it with the Anglo-Saxon colonization of America, based on the containment or eventual elimination of the Indians instead of their assimilation or incorporation in colonial society, to realize that, to a great extent, the Spanish organization of a multiethnic society was a unique, although hardly perfect, achievement."[78]

Though the technological and cultural dominance of the Spaniards dictated the evolution of New World societies from California to Chile, miscegenation and the reciprocal influences between Spaniards, Indians, and African slaves created an Afro-Latin America in the islands of the Caribbean and a mestizo America in Mexico and Peru. Spanish culture predominated in northern Mexico and the present-day U.S. Southwest, but even Juan de Oñate's son was a mixture of Spanish and Indian, Basque on his father's side and a descendant of Montezuma on his mother's side.[79] In the West Indies, the importation of African slaves provided the labor force for sugar cane production and stock raising, and this trade between 1510 and 1550 produced a preponderance of blacks over the Spanish population. The royal chronicler Oviedo wrote in the 1540s that Africans had been brought to Hispaniola in such large numbers that the land appeared to be a replica of Ethiopia.[80]

Horses, hogs, sheep, burros, goats, and cattle imported from Spain multiplied rapidly in the New World. These animals were soon transported to the Caribbean mainland and Mexico. Following the conquest of Mexico and the discovery of rich silver mines in the north, the flow of men and animals to Zacatecas and other mining communities accelerated. Settlement of the north created a demand for agricultural goods and beef and mutton. Spaniards in search of precious metals continued to press northward, and in 1598 the last *adelantado* of the New World, Don Juan de Oñate, took possession of the land of New Mexico.

Cattle and sheep arrived with Oñate's colonists. Although *mestas*, powerful sheep raisers' corporations originating in Spain and found elsewhere in the Spanish colonies, were not established in New Mexico, it appears that "the powerful stockgrowers' associations which played such an important role in the trans-Mississippi West were patterned after New Spain's Mesta."[81] By 1827 there were 240,000 sheep in New Mexico, and in 1849 sheep were first driven from this region to the California goldfields. (One individual who was active in the transporting of sheep to California was Manuel Alvarez, native of Spain, holder of Mexican passports, and U.S. consul in Santa Fe. Fluent in Spanish, English, and French, this merchant and stock raiser was a prominent politician and led the statehood movement in New Mexico following the U.S. conquest.)[82] In California and in northwestern New Mexico, the coarse-wooled *churros* were crossbred with *merino* rams, and in the latter half of the nineteenth century this improved breed was used as foundation stock in the establishment of the sheep industry in the Far West, the Rocky Mountains, and the Great Plains.[83]

Cattle were introduced into Mexico soon after its conquest, and their "sudden multiplication is one of the most astonishing biological phenomena observable in the New World."[84] Creole longhorns were driven north to feed the miners of the silver bonanzas in the last half of the sixteenth century, but soon the ranching frontier expanded beyond the mining frontier. By the 1820s ranchers in Texas owned 100,000 cattle; by 1846 these had multiplied fourfold and had a value of $1.5 million. Texas cattle were introduced into Colorado, and in

1869 a million longhorns grazed in this region, along "with a considerable number of sheep."[85]

Cattle, sheep, horses, and swine were raised in California by the Franciscan friars and their Indian charges, but California's pastoral era truly began after the secularization of the missions. During the Mexican period and until the 1860s, the rancho, with its "cattle on a thousand hills," was the principal economic unit. Before 1848 cattle were valued only for their hides and tallow, but after the war with Mexico the beef trade began. The longhorn, "once worth a dollar or two for its skin and fat, rose in value to $70 in 1849, when it became eating fare for the miners." By 1870 Anglo lawyers, squatters, and drought made for the transfer of the great landed estates to new owners, and many ranchers and *californio* cowboys became sheep-shearers.[86] Not only were most cowboys in 1870 Hispanics, but the cowboy culture of the Southwest venerated in John Wayne movies is Spanish-Mexican in origin. It was only when the Anglo-American crossed the Mississippi and appropriated such items as the lariat, the sombrero, the mustang, and the tall-horned range saddle that he was transformed from pioneer into cavalier, from squatter into buckaroo, from Midwestern farmer into "a yearning nation's blue-eyed pride."[87]

Indians were also influenced materially and spiritually by Spanish-Mexican contact. Pueblo Indians in New Mexico adopted Spanish ovens (*hornos*), wooden plows, two-wheeled carts, iron axes, saws, and other utensils, as well as new animals such as the domestic chicken, the cat, and the horse.[88] Hispanic and intertribal trade at Taos made for a frontier outpost where cultures fused. Even more spectacular was the equestrian revolution witnessed on the Plains. The economy and culture of the Plains Indians were altered into new configurations when pedestrian people were transformed into "feather-streaming, buffalo-chasing, wild-raising, recklessly fighting Indians."[89]

American agriculture also had its beginnings in Spain's New World possessions. The chief money crop shipped to Spain in the 1540s was sugar, which rivaled stock raising as an industry.[90] Sugar cane cultivation rapidly spread to the mainland and eventually reached Texas and Louisiana. Mexican wheat, first planted by the African Juan Garrido, was being exported to the West Indies and Tierra Firme as early as 1535,[91] and the wheats grown in California in the latter half of the eighteenth century had been tested over the centuries and quickly adapted to that state's climate. Prior to 1860, only the mission grape was grown in California; in the same period the El Paso area had many vineyards, and the wines and brandy of the New Mexican southern district were famous.[92] Other fruits introduced by the friars into the Southwest were oranges, apples, figs, apricots, peaches, pomegranates, pears, and limes. Finally, a superior Mexican cotton "replaced almost completely all other varieties" in the southern United States after 1806.[93]

Moreover, miners in the West "turned for advice to those same Latin American veterans who were so often their instructors in the art of mining." Mexican ordinances and the Spanish Continental Mining Code were drawn upon for California usage, and "more than one Anglo-Saxon acquired his first knowledge of gold mining by working alongside a Chilean or Mexican in the Sierra foothills."[94] Spanish words such as *placer, bonanza, escoria,* and *xacal* were soon a part of mining vocabulary, as was the *patio* process (the amalgamation of silver with mercury), introduced into Mexico by Bartolomé de Medina in 1556.

The search for great wealth in the lands north of Mexico City served as the impetus for the colonization of New Mexico. However, because the utopian dream of spiritual conquest envisioned by mendicant friars and their friends was supported by the crown, colonial expansion north from Mexico was often undertaken by friars acting as agents of both church and state. Conquest of the Aztecs, Chichimecas, Pueblos, and other Indian groups was followed by the establishment of military garrisons, civil settlements, missions, and the spread of the Gospel and Spanish ways. Although the mission schools were rather modest, they taught the Indians "both the basics of the three R's and instruction in the manual trades."[95]

One outstanding missionary was Father Eusebio Francisco Kino, who arrived in northern Sonora in 1687. By 1700 he had extended the mission settlements into southern Arizona, where he taught the Pima Indians to raise wheat, corn, and cattle and imparted the arts of carpentry, weaving, and blacksmithing. Known as "the padre on horseback," Father Kino served as missionary, explorer, builder, trailbreaker, cattleman, and Indian agent. He never owned more than two shirts in the twenty-four years that he served on the northwestern frontier of New Spain.

Through the efforts of the missionaries, Indians were incorporated into Spanish communities. The best example of an area that witnessed race mixture between Spaniards and Indians but that remained culturally and institutionally Spanish is New Mexico. As

France V. Scholes demonstrated in his pioneering studies of New Mexico's colonial period, there was no social distinction between Spaniards and Creoles in seventeenth-century New Mexico, and "the position of the half-castes in New Mexico was undoubtedly better than in the more densely settled areas of New Spain. Life on the frontier put men on their own, and if a mestizo made a good soldier he was a welcome member of the community. Many of them attained high military rank, and some became alcaldes mayores or members of the cabildo of Santa Fe."[96] In short, it was impossible to estimate the proportions of Spaniards, Creoles, and castes in the colony because social distinctions were blurred, so over a period of time all colonists professed allegiance to the group that defended the colony and upheld Spanish traditions on the frontier.

The original settlers of New Mexico were "ordinary military and pastoral people, good folks in the main, who were neither peons nor convicts."[97] But those who arrived with Oñate were granted "the title of nobility with a *solar conocido*" once they had "settled the land and complied with their treaty." Though recognized as hidalgos, New Mexico's farmers and stock raisers were rustic provincials in their rural ways. But like all products of Western civilization, they felt the tyranny of time's winged chariot, as denoted by the rock sundial erected in the main plaza of Santa Fe in the 1820s. The structure is inscribed *Vita fugit sicut umbra*; the line, taken from Job 14:2, states that man "cometh forth like a flower, and is cut down; he fleeth also as a shadow, and continueth not."[98]

Native New Mexicans continued to practice acculturation and assimilation into the nineteenth century, as demonstrated by the genealogy of Don José González, *vecino* of Ranchos de Taos, a great buffalo hunter and briefly the governor of New Mexico in 1837. González, the son of genízaros and the grandson of a Frenchman and a Plains Indian woman, was a child of citizens living at San Francisco del Rancho who had been reared in Spanish homes, adopted Spanish ways of living, and became "Spaniards." His brothers and sisters married into Spanish families of the Rio Arriba region; one of his relatives, named María de los Santos González, was married to Marcos Vigil, the legitimate son of Miguel Antonio Vigil and María Paula Antonia Abeyta, by Father Gabriel Ussel on March 7, 1859, in the church of Our Lady of Guadalupe of Don Fernando de Taos.[99]

On July 22, 1870, the ninth census for New Mexico, Subdivision No. 1, County of Taos, listed the inhabitants of Ranchos de Taos.

Marcos Vigil was described as a thirty-three-year-old white male farmer whose real estate was estimated at $425. Born in New Mexico in about 1837, Marcos Vigil could not write. His wife, Santos (María Santos González Vigil), was a twenty-seven-year-old white female born in the territory of New Mexico who could neither read nor write. Their son Urbano (José Urbano) was eight years old.[100]

In the 1870s the Vigil family moved to Las Animas County, Colorado, and founded the plaza settlement of Vigil. There José Urbano Vigil began his career as a schoolteacher, and prior to 1900 he became postmaster at Vigil. In addition to his business ventures, which including ranching, farming, merchandising, land speculation, stagecoach commerce, and publishing, he served as county commissioner (1892–95), county clerk for three successiveterms, delegate to the Democratic National Convention in 1908, state license inspector for Las Animas County from 1909 to 1913, and postmaster at Trinidad, Colorado, in 1913. He held the last office until his death in 1915. He was buried in Vigil Cemetery, now surrounded by "isolated plazas, reminders of thriving communities and a pattern of life that formed an important part of an earlier southwestern culture."[101]

Before these thriving communities became history and their inhabitants became a subordinate ethnic group in the new Great Plains of railroads, commercial progress, and rapidly growing cities, cultural and genetic interchange continued in this multiethnic society. In the early years of the American occupation, Kit Carson, Charles Bent, James Bowie, Antonio Leroux, Charles Beaubien, Céran St. Vrain, George Storz, John Lawrence, Abel Stearns, Simeon Hart, and countless others in Texas, Arizona, California, and New Mexico married into Spanish-surnamed families. A check in ethnic fusion, caused in part by the arrival of newly arrived European immigrants, took place between 1885 and 1920. In recent years intermarriage and ethnic fusion have become commonplace among the Hispanos of southern Colorado and New Mexico, and "marriages of second- and third-generation in Los Angeles are assimilationist."[102] It thus appears that Hispanics, whether recent arrivals or charter-member early Americans, will gradually mix with members of other ethnic groups; they are genetically and culturally like every son and daughter of the Americas, heirs to the whole world, with their roots being rooted in change.

The Hispanic presence in the Great Plains may be viewed in a number of ways. It is as old as the region's sixteenth-century exploration and as young as the recent movement of Central and South

Americans, Puerto Ricans, Cubans, and Spanish-surnamed South-westerners to the Midwest. Change, continuity, diversity, and unity characterize Hispanic history and culture, and Spanish-surnamed persons on the Plains and elsewhere have been designated by different names. An example is the term "Hispanic," which became "acceptable as a label that symbolized a realignment in political directions." This term "presumed decreasing identification with ethnicity but a continued acknowledgment of being Mexican American" or having cultural roots in Latin America.[103]

Regardless of their origins, Hispanic images, numbers, and ways increasingly blend with the ingredients that form the cultural landscape of America's heartland. Hispanic influences are as prosaic as burritos and the soap operas on the lone Spanish-language TV channel in Lincoln, Nebraska; they are as profound as an interpretation of César Vallejo's images of death or Richard Wilbur's evocation of "holy things" done "for love and in all weathers."[104] Given their past, their numbers, and the reality of greater America, Hispanics in the Great Plains will multiply, accommodating and contributing to the shared culture of this "New World."

Notes

1. Leonard Pitt, *The Decline of the Californios: A Social History of the Spanish-Speaking Californians, 1846-1890* (Berkeley: University of California Press, 1971), p. 291.

2. Charles Gibson, ed., *The Black Legend: Anti-Spanish Attitudes in the Old World and the New* (New York: Alfred A. Knopf, 1971), pp. 32, 64.

3. Brian R. Hamnett, review of Philip Wayne Powell, *Tree of Hate: Propaganda and Prejudices Affecting United States Relations with the Hispanic World*, in *Hispanic American Historical Review* 53 (November 1973): 671–72.

4. Quoted by Magnus Mörner, *Race Mixture in the History of Latin America* (Boston: Little, Brown and Co., 1967), p. 86.

5. Thomas E. Skidmore and Peter H. Smith, *Modern Latin America* (New York: Oxford University Press, 1989), p. 4. Although the poll cited by the authors was conducted in 1940 by the Office of Public Opinion Research, it is doubtful whether the stereotypes have changed. In fact,

these images have probably hardened but are disguised as "Hispanic color and spirit."

6.   "Its Your Turn in the Sun," *Time* 125 (October 16, 1978): 48–61.

7.   F. D. Bean, E. H. Stephen, and W. Opits, "The Mexican Origin Population in the United States: A Demographic Overview," in Rodolfo O. de la Garza, et. al., eds., *The Mexican American Experience: An Interdisciplinary Anthology* (Austin: University of Texas Press, 1985), pp. 57–75.

8.   Sharon Cohen, "Hispanics Invade Midwest to Pursue American Dream," *Lincoln [NE] Journal-Star* (August 4, 1991). The AP article noted that "southwest Iowa and parts of Nebraska, Minnesota, Kansas, and Ohio are turning into the promised land for thousands of Hispanics finding work in factories, hospitals, food-processing companies and, very often, meatpacking plants."

9.   Ibid. "Nebraska's Hispanic population increased 31.9 percent during the 1980s, compared with a decline of 0.7 percent for the white population."

10.   Ibid.

11.   Ibid.

12.   David J. de Levita, *The Concept of Identity* (New York: Basic Books, 1967), p. 7.

13.   For Hispanophobia and its development, see Philip Wayne Powell, *Tree of Hate: Propaganda and Prejudices Affecting United States Relations with the Hispanic World* (New York: Basic Books, 1971).

14.   Leslie Fiedler, *Waiting for the End* (New York: Stein and Day, 1970), p. 71.

15.   Herman Melville, *The Confidence-Man: His Masquerade*, ed. Hershel Parker (New York: W. W. Norton & Co., 1971), pp. 124–31. See also Robert A. Trennert, "Popular Imagery and the American Indian: A Centennial View," *New Mexico Historical Review* 51 (July 1976): 215–32, and Roy Harvey Pearce, "The Metaphysics of Indian-Hating," *Ethnohistory* 4 (Spring 1957): 27–40.

16.   Winthrop Jordan, *White Over Black: American Attitudes Toward the Negro, 1550–1812* (Chapel Hill: University of North Carolina Press, 1968).

17.   John A. Garraty, *The American Nation: A History of the United States* (New York: Harper & Row Publishers, 1966), p. 375. See also Alphonso

Pinkney, *Black Americans* (Englewood Cliffs, NJ: Prentice-Hall, Inc., 1974).

18. Cecil Robinson, *With the Ears of Strangers: The Mexican in American Literature* (Tucson: University of Arizona Press, 1963).

19. Fiedler, *Waiting for the End*, p. 125.

20. Robinson, *With the Ears of Strangers*, p. vii.

21. Ibid., pp. 69, 72.

22. Quoted by Jack D. Forbes (ed.), *The Indian in America's Past* (Englewood Cliffs, NJ: Prentice-Hall, Inc., 1964), p. 17. As Robinson notes, even General Santa Anna was called "that yaller nigger" in S. Hammett's *Piney Woods Tavern* (1858). See Robinson, *With the Ears of Strangers*, p. 71.

23. John P. Bloom, "New Mexicans Viewed by Anglo-Americans," *New Mexico Historical Review* 34 (July 1959): 165–98.

24. Robinson, *With the Ears of Strangers*, p. 73.

25. Josiah Gregg, *Commerce of the Prairies*, ed. Max L. Moorhead (Norman: University of Oklahoma Press, 1954), p. 106.

26. Lewis H. Garrard, *Wah-to-yah and the Taos Trail*, with an introduction by A. B. Guthrie, Jr. (Norman: University of Oklahoma Press, 1955), pp. 171, 181.

27. David Lavender, *Bent's Fort* (Garden City, NY: Doubleday & Co., Inc., 1954), p. 176.

28. Carey McWilliams, *North from Mexico: The Spanish-Speaking People of the United States*, rev. ed., updated by Matt S. Meier (New York: Praeger, 1990), p. 71. George Sánchez observed that families in New Mexico were closely interrelated and that "field hands, herders, and other laborers, as well as domestic servants, were often close relatives of the *patrón*. Nearly all were land holders, with virtually the same economic standards of living as their employer." See *Forgotten People, A Study of New Mexicans* (Albuquerque: Calvin Horn, Publisher, Inc., 1967), p. 6. Nancie L. González is of the opinion that until late in New Mexico's history, social relations were egalitarian and there were "no *patrones* in the true sense of the word." Nancie L. González, *The Spanish-Americans of New Mexico: A Heritage of Pride* (Albuquerque: University of New Mexico Press, 1969), p. 45.

29. See "'Mexican American' and 'Chicano': Emerging Terms for a People Coming of Age," in Norris Hundley, Jr., ed., *The Chicano* (Santa Barbara: Clio Books, 1975), pp. 143–60.

30. Pitt, *The Decline of the Californios*, p. 53.

31. "The total cost to the federal government of the World War II bracero program amounted to more than $450 per bracero, or more than $113 million." Matt S. Meier and Feliciano Rivera, *The Chicanos: A History of Mexican Americans* (New York: Hill and Wang, 1972), p. 207.

32. Joan W. Moore with Harry Pachon, *Mexican Americans* (Englewood Cliffs, NJ: Prentice-Hall, Inc., 1976), pp. 65–66.

33. *Midwest Hispanic Network Newsletter* 4:2 (March 1990).

34. Donald Cutter, "Foreword," in Oakah L. Jones, Jr., ed., *The Spanish Borderlands — A First Reader* (Los Angeles: Lorrin L. Morrison, 1974), pp. vii–ix. The chapters in this book first appeared as articles in *Journal of the West*.

35. Arthur M. Corwin, "Mexican-American History: An Assessment," *Pacific Historical Review* 42 (August 1973): 269–308.

36. McWilliams, *North from Mexico*, p. 7.

37. Ibid., p. 8. "No matter how sharply the Spanish-speaking may differ among themselves over the question of nomenculture, the sense of cleavage from or opposition to the Anglos has always been an important factor in their lives and it is this feeling which gives cohesion to the group."

38. Alfredo Jiménez Núñez, *Los hispanos de Nuevo México: Contribución a una antropología de la cultura hispana en USA*, vol. 12 (Sevilla: Serie Publicaciones del Seminario de Antropología Americana, 1974), p. 141.

39. Richard L. Nostrand, "Comment in Reply" to Niles Hansen's "Commentary" in *Annals*, Association of American Geographers 71 (1981): 282–83; Moore, *Mexican Americans*, p. 136.

40. Herbert Marcuse, *One-Dimensional Man* (Boston: Beacon Press, 1966), p. 8.

41. For Tijerina, see Peter Nabokov, *Tijerina and the Courthouse Raid* (Albuquerque: University of New Mexico Press, 1970).

42. Rubén Cobos, *A Dictionary of New Mexico and Southern Colorado Spanish* (Santa Fe: Museum of New Mexico Press, 1983), pp. xii and 105.

43. Ibid., p. xv.

44. As my friend Professor Cobos notes, "It is very likely that by the turn of the twenty-first century English and Mexican Spanish will have completely replaced the archaic local Spanish dialect." Ibid., p. xvi.

45. See J. Allen Williams, Jr., David R. Johnson, and Miguel A. Carranza, "Ethnic Assimilation and Pluralism in Nebraska," in Frederick C. Luebke, ed. *Ethnicity on the Great Plains* (Lincoln: University of Nebraska, 1980), pp. 210–29.

46. Ralph H. Vigil, "The New Borderlands History: A Critique," *New Mexico Historical Review* 48 (July 1973), footnote 11.

47. Terry G. Jordan, review of John Haddox, *Los Chicanos, An Awakening People*, in *Southwestern Historical Quarterly* 75 (July 1971): 116–17.

48. Moore, *Mexican Americans*, p. 151.

49. Ibid., pp. 133–35.

50. Ibid., p. 121.

51. Michael Maccoby, "On Mexican National Character," *Annals of the American Academy of Political and Social Science* 370 (March 1967): 63–73. See also Eleanor Burke Leacock, ed., *The Culture of Poverty: A Critique* (New York, 1971).

52. See Frank G. Mittelbach and Joan W. Moore, "Ethnic Endogamy — The Case of Mexican Americans," in John H. Burma, ed., *Mexican Americans in the United States* (Cambridge, MA: Schenkman Publishing Co., 1970), pp. 235–48; Leo Grebler, et. al., *The Mexican-American People: The Nation's Second Largest Minority* (New York: The Free Press, 1970), pp. 378–99; Moore, *Mexican Americans*, p. 160.

53. Felix M. Padilla, "On the Nature of Latino Ethnicity," in Rodolfo O. de la Garza, et.al., *Mexican American Experiences*, pp. 322–45.

54. Ibid., pp. 334–35, 343.

55. Ibid., p. 339.

56. David J. Weber, *The Mexican Frontier, 1821–1846: The American Southwest Under Mexico* (Albuquerque: University of New Mexico, 1982).

57. "In Defence of Columbus: The Trouble with Eden," *The Economist* (December 21, 1991–January 3, 1992), pp. 73–77.

58. In their struggle for independence, Mexican creoles (Spaniards born in America) cultivated the nationalist cult of Mexican antiquity and came to call themselves Americans after 1780. But when a conservative Mexico gained independence from a liberal Spain in 1821, Mexican politicians soon viewed Mexico's Indian past with either indifference or outright hostility. The study of ancient Mexico did continue, however, as did the debate between the defenders and detractors of conquest and colonization. See Benjamin Keen, *The Aztec Image in Western Thought* (New Brunswick, NJ: Rutgers University Press, 1971), pp. 316–27; Howard F. Cline, vol. ed., *Guide to Ethnohistorical Sources*, Part 1, in R. Wauchope, ed., *Handbook of Middle American Indians* (Austin: University of Texas Press, 1972), 12: 13.

59. In 1945 José Clemente Orozco wrote: "We are continously classifying ourselves as Indians, creoles, or mestizos, thinking only of the mixture of bloods, as though we were dealing with race horses, and from this system of classification parties have arisen saturated with hatred, which are engaged in a life struggle, the indigenists and the Hispanists." See "Art and Politics in Mexico," in Lewis Hanke, *Mexico and the Caribbean* (Princeton, NJ: Princeton University Press, 1967), pp. 238–40.

60. Oakah L. Jones, Jr., "Introduction," in *The Spanish Borderlands — A First Reader*, pp. 2–3; John Francis Bannon, ed., *Bolton and the Spanish Borderlands* (Norman: University of Oklahoma Press, 1964), p. 303. The Spanish borderlands were made an enduring and accepted part of the American story largely by Herbert Eugene Bolton, a student of Frederick Jackson Turner. The Bolton approach encompassed all the Americas. Bolton's many students continued his work, and the result has been a greater understanding of the history of the Americas and the borderlands. A knowledge of this "other frontier" has led to the realization that "the Anglo-American experience, magnificent and thrilling though it was, actually was not quite as unique as it is sometimes pictured and chauvinistically thought to be. The Anglo-American frontier can be better understood and more properly evaluated by process of comparison." John Francis Bannon, *The Spanish Americas: The Colonial Americas,* vol. 1 (New York: McGraw-Hill, 1952), pp. 1–17.

61. John Francis Bannon, ed., *Bolton and the Spanish Borderlands*, p. 303.

62. H. G. Koenigsberger and George L. Mosse, *Europe in the Sixteenth Century* (New York: Holt, Rinehart and Winston, 1968), p. 94.

63. Lesley Byrd Simpson, *Many Mexicos* (Berkeley: University of California Press, 1959), p. 25.

64. Lewis Hanke, *The Spanish Struggle for Justice in the Conquest of America* (Boston: Little, Brown & Co., 1965), p. 1.

65. For the life of Las Casas (1474?–1566), see Henry Raup Wagner with Helen Rand Parish, *The Life and Writings of Bartolomé de las Casas*, (Albuquerque: University of New Mexico Press, 1967).

66. Gibson, *The Black Legend*, p. 14–15.

67. For the contrast between the historical Martínez and the figure found in *Death Comes for the Archbishop*, see Ralph H. Vigil, "Willa Cather and Historical Reality," *New Mexico Historical Review* 50 (April 1975): 123–38.

68. Arnold Toynbee, *A Study of History*, 13 vols. (London: Oxford University Press, 1934–61), 1: xvii, 211–49; Bannon, *The Spanish Borderlands Frontier*, p. 5.

69. C. E. Marshall, "The Birth of the Mestizo in New Spain," *Hispanic American Historical Review* 19 (May 1939): 161–84.

70. Magnus Mörner, *Race Mixture in the History of Latin America* (Boston: Little, Brown & Co., 1967), p. 45; Gonzalo Aguirre Beltrán, "The Integration of the Negro into the National Society of Mexico," in Magnus Mörner, ed., *Race and Class in Latin America* (New York: Columbia University Press, 1970), pp. 11–27.

71. Hubert Howe Bancroft, *History of Arizona and New Mexico, 1530–1888*, reprint (Albuquerque: University of New Mexico Press, 1962), pp. 279–82; Fray Angélico Chávez, "The Penitentes of New Mexico," *New Mexico Historical Review* 29 (April 1954): 97–123; Angel Rosenblat, *La población indigena y el mestizaje en América*, 2vols. (Buenos Aires: Editorial Nova, 1954), 2: 135–45.

72. H. Bailey Carroll and J. Villasana Haggard, eds., *Three New Mexico Chronicles* (Albuquerque: Quivira Society, 1942), pp. 8–9; Oakah L. Jones, Jr., *Los Paisanos: Spanish Settlers on the Northern Plains of New Spain* (Norman: University of Oklahoma, 1979), pp. 131–32.

73. Pitt, *The Decline of the Californios*, p. 13.

74. Jack Forbes, "Black Pioneers: The Spanish-Speaking Afro-American of the Southwest," in George E. Frakes and Curtis B. Salberg, eds., *Minorities in California History* (New York: Random House, 1971), pp. 20–33.

75. Jack Holmes, "Spanish Influence," in David C. Roller and Robert W. Twyman, eds., *The Encyclopedia of Southern History* (Baton Rouge: Louisiana State University Press, 1979); John Francis McDermott, ed.,

The Spanish in the Mississippi Valley, 1762–1804 (Urbana: University of Illinois Press, 1974), pp. 272–308.

76.   Information received from Professor Vicenta Cortés Alonso, friend and author of "Geopolítica del sureste de los Estados Unidos (1750-1800)," *Revista de Indias*, 12: 47 (1952): 23–49.

77.   McDermott, *The Spanish in the Mississippi Valley*, p. 24.

78.   Jacques Lafaye and James Lockhart, "A Scholarly Debate: The Origins of Modern Mexico — Indígenistas vs. Hispanistas," *The Americas* 48 (January 1992): 315–30.

79.   Cristóbal de Oñate, the son of the founder of New Mexico, was briefly interim governor. Don Pedro de Peralta was appointed governor and captain-general of New Mexico in 1609. See Marc Simmons, *The Last Conquistador: Juan de Oñate and the Settling of the Far Southwest* (Norman: University of Oklahoma Press, 1991), pp. 181–82.

80.   Ralph H. Vigil, "Negro Slaves and Rebels in the Spanish Possessions, 1503–1558," *The Historian* 33 (August 1971): 637–55.

81.   Keith W. Algier, ed., "The Puebla Mesta Ordinances of 1556 and 1560," *New Mexico Historical Review* 44 (January 1969): 5–24.

82.   Thomas E. Chávez, *Manuel Alvarez, 1794–1856: A Southwestern Biography* (Boulder: University Press of Colorado, 1990), pp. 167–74.

83.   Alvar Ward Carlson, "New Mexico's Sheep Industry," *New Mexico Historical Review* 44 (January 1969): 25–49; Harry Bernstein, "Spanish Influences in the United States: Economic Aspects," *Hispanic American Historical Review* 18 (February 1938): 43–65.

84.   François Chevalier, *Land and Society in Colonial Mexico: The Great Hacienda* (Berkeley: University of California Press, 1970), p. 93. In the 1590s, "a single individual, Juan Nieto, a Mexico City contractor had possessed enough hides to lose 80,000 of them at one blow in a ship wreck." Ibid., p. 107.

85.   H. Bernstein, "Spanish Influences in the United States," p. 46.

86.   Pitt, *The Decline of the Californios*, pp. 12, 108, 254.

87.   "The Mexican cowboy's influence was so widespread that it impressed his American counterpart in the last century, who took over his rodeo, saddle, stirrups (Andalusian in origin), huge spurs, apparel, and even, in all likelihood, character traits." Chevalier, *Land and Society in Colonial Mexico*, p. 114.

88.   Charles H. Lange, *Cochiti, A New Mexico Pueblo, Past and Present* (Carbondale: Southern Illinois University Press, 1968), p. 90; Edwin R. Embree, *Indians of the Americas* (New York: Collier Books, 1970), p. 216.

89.   William Brandon, *The American Heritage Book of Indians* (New York: Simon and Schuster, 1974), p. 305. See also Peter Farb, *Man's Rise to Civilization* (New York: Dutton, 1971), pp. 145–68; Francis Haines, "Where did the Plains Indians get Their Horses," *American Anthropologist* 40 (January–March 1938): 112–17; Clark Wissler, "The Influence of the Horse in the Development of Plains Cultures," *American Anthropologist* 16 (January–March 1914): 1–25.

90.   G. A. Mejía Ricart, *Historia de Santo Domingo*, 5 vols. to date (Ciudad Trujillo: Pol. Hnos., 1948–54), 5: 207.

91.   Arthur P. Whitaker, "Spanish Contributions to American Agriculture," *Agricultural History* 3 (January 1929): 1–14.

92.   Bancroft, *History of Arizona and New Mexico*, p. 276.

93.   H. Bernstein, "Spanish Influences in the United States," p. 53. Bernstein notes that the Mexican seed, free of disease and having a larger yield, was second only to the invention of the cotton gin in increasing cotton production.

94.   Rodman W. Paul, *California Gold* (Lincoln: University of Nebraska Press, 1969), pp. 48, 213.

95.   Bannon, *The Spanish Borderlands Frontier*, p. 71. See also Pius Joseph Barth, *Franciscan Education and the Social Order in the Spanish North America (1502–1821), A Dissertation* (Chicago: The University of Chicago, 1945).

96.   France V. Scholes, "Civil Government and Society in New Mexico in the Seventeenth Century," *New Mexico Historical Review* 10 (April 1935): 71–111.

97.   Fray Angélico Chávez, *Origins of New Mexico Families* (Santa Fe: The Historical Society of New Mexico, 1954), p. xv.

98.   H. Bailey Carroll and J. Villasana Haggard, *Three New Mexico Chronicles*, p. 85.

99.   Fray Angélico Chávez, "José Gonzales, Genízaro Governor," *New Mexico Historical Review* 30 (July 1955): 190–94; Declaration for Widow's Pension of Mrs. María Santos G. Vigil, December 19, 1902, Military Service Records, National Archives (GSA), Pension File WC 670 544.

100. Ninth Census for New Mexico, Subdivision No. 1, County of Taos, *State Records Center, Santa Fe, New Mexico.* The 1850 Census for Ranchos de Taos states that Marcos Vigil, an eleven-year-old white male, was the son of Miguel Antonio Vigil, a forty-nine-year-old white farmer born in Río Arriba, and María Antonio Abeita, Miguel Antonio's forty-two-year-old wife. Miguel Antonio Vigil's real estate was valued at $100. The couples' three other children were eighteen-year-old Juan Antonio, a laborer; sixteen-year-old María Marcelina; and fourteen-year-old José Urbano. All of the children had been born in Taos County (National Archives Microfilm Publication, No. 432). The 1860 Census states that Family 755 in Ranchos de Taos consisted of sixty-six-year-old Miguel Antonio Vigil, twenty-one-year-old Marcos Vigil, and Santos González. Miguel Antonio's real estate was estimated at $400; his personal estate was valued at $600.

101. *Chronicle News* (Trinidad, CO), June 3, 1915; William B. Taylor and Elliott West, "Patrón Leadership at the Crossroads: Southern Colorado in the Late Nineteenth Century," *Pacific Historical Review* 42 (August 1973): 335–57.

102. Mittelbach and Moore, "Ethnic Endogamy — The Case of Mexican Americans," in Burma, *Mexican-Americans*, p. 239.

103. Arnoldo DeLeón, *Mexican Americans in Texas: A Brief History* (Arlington Heights, IL: Harlan Davidson, Inc., 1993), p. 137.

104. Edmundo Bendezú, "Vision española de la muerte según Vallejo," *Hispania* 72 (1989): 55–58; Richard Wilbur, "A Plain Song for Comadre," in *New Collected Poems* (San Diego, New York, London: A Harvest/HBJ/ Book, 1989), p. 244.

Authors and Editors

FÉLIX D. ALMARÁZ, JR. is professor of history at the University of Texas at San Antonio. He is the author of *Tragic Cavalier: Governor Manuel Salcedo of Texas, 1808–1813* (Austin: University of Texas Press, 1971); *Long Upon the Land: The San Antonio Missions and Their System of Land Tenure* (Austin: University of Texas Press, 1988); and *Empty Echoes in a Howling Wind: Myths and Realities in the Tejano Community, from Cabeza de Vaca to Santa Anna* (El Paso: University of Texas at El Paso Press, 1986). He edited a special issue of the *Journal of the West* (April 1985) devoted to borderlands history and has written numerous articles.

THOMAS E. CHÁVEZ is director of the Palace of the Governors of the Museum of New Mexico in Santa Fe. He is the author of *Manuel Alvarez, A Biography* (College Station: Texas A&M Press, 1991) and, forthcoming with Fray Angelico Chávez, *Wake for a Fat Vicar: A Biography of Father Jose Manuel Ortiz* (William Gannon Press). He edited *New Mexico in the Gilded Age* (Albuquerque: University of New Mexico Press, 1992) and has curated numerous exhibits at the Palace of the Governors, including "New Mexico in the Gilded Age, 1880–1900" and "18th Century Mexican Religious Art and New Mexico Santos."

FRANCES W. KAYE is editor of the *Great Plains Quarterly* and professor of English at the University of Nebraska–Lincoln. She has published numerous articles about Great Plains literature, especially concerning the contrasts between Canadian and American themes. She co-edited *Mapping the North American Plains: Essays in the History of Cartography* (Norman: University of Oklahoma Press, 1987), and is the author of *Isolation and Masquerade: Willa Cather's Women* (New York: Peter Lang Publishers, 1993).

RUSSELL M. MAGNAGHI is professor of history at Northern Michigan University. He has edited and written an introduction to *The Hasinais* by Herbert Eugene Bolton (Norman: University of Oklahoma Press, 1987) and *From the Mississippi to the Pacific: Essays in Honor of John Francis Bannon* (Marquette, MI: Northern Michigan University Press, 1982). Forthcoming is *Indian Servitude, Labor, Slavery and Captivity in the Americas: A Critical Bibliography*, to be published by Scarecrow Press.

RALPH H. VIGIL is professor of history and ethnic studies at the University of Nebraska–Lincoln. He is the author of *Alonso de Zorita, Royal Judge and Christian Humanist, 1512–1585* (Norman: University of Oklahoma Press, 1987) and numerous articles, including "Bartolomé de Las Casas, Judge Alonso de Zorita, and the Franciscans: A Collaborative Effort for the Spiritual Conquest of the Borderlands," *The Americas* 38 (July 1981): 45–57; "The Heritage of the Spanish Borderlands: A Review Essay," *Red River Valley Historical Review* 2 (Fall 1975): 413–20; "The New Borderlands History: A Critique," *New Mexico Historical Review* 48 (July 1973): 189–208; and "Inequality and Ideology in Borderlands Historiography," *Latin American Research Review* 29 (Number 1, 1994): 155–71.

WALDO R. WEDEL is senior archaeologist emeritus of the United States National Museum. He is the author of *Prehistoric Man on the Great Plains* (Norman: University of Oklahoma Press, 1961); *Central Plains Prehistory: Holocene Environments and Culture Change in the Republican River Basin* (Lincoln: University of Nebraska Press, 1986) and numerous other articles and books on Great Plains archaeology.

JOHN R. WUNDER is professor of history and director of the Center for Great Plains Studies. He authored *"Retained by the People": A History of American Indians and the Bill of Rights* (New York: Oxford University, 1994), *The Kiowa* (New York: Chelsea House Publishers, 1989), and numerous articles, including "Frontier Conspiracy: Law, History, Turner, and the Cordova Rebellion," *Red River Valley Historical Review* 7 (Summer 1982): 51–67, with Rebecca J. Herring. He also edited *At Home on the Range: Essays on the History of Western Social and Domestic Life* (Westport, CT: Greenwood Press, 1985) and *Working the Range: Essays on the History of Western Land Management and the Environment* (Westport, CT: Greenwood Press, 1985).

Index